Contact Annual of Photographers · 6th Edition

★
ELFANDE

copyright © 1989
Barry O'Dwyer
Nicholas Gould

ISBN NO 1 870458 11 7

2

**The Contact Book
of Photographers
Annual**

Publishers
Nicholas Gould
Barry O'Dwyer

Published by
Elfande Art Publishing
Unit 39
Bookham Industrial Park
Church St
Bookham Surrey
KT23 3EU

Telephone 0372 59559
Fax   0372 59699

Cover Photography
Ross Feltus

Photography
this spread
by Michael Hoppen

Agency: Publitek Ltd
Client: Duphar Laboratories

Printed in Holland
by Royal Smeets Offset

Production Director
Nicholas Gould

Production Assistant
Nadia Gargani

Graphic Reproduction
by Laser at
Studio North Ltd

Sales executive
Nicky Dompsey

Research & Administration
Zoe Biggs

**Edited & Designed by
Barry O'Dwyer**

Editorial

Following the publication of this annual, the same two questions arise each year. The first is, how do people show their work and secondly, are we their agents. Contact is a paid for directory. That is, each person showing their work pays to have their work printed within either the Photographers or Illustrators section of the publication. Apart from the work, participants also have the opportunity to give a brief resume of work undertaken, clients, etc. This method of advertising enables work shown to be viewed by a much wider audience than the limited circle of contacts that each person appearing in the book has. Perhaps, more importantly, it often leads to projects that offer a fresh challenge due to the books diverse distribution. This 'Silent Salesman' approach enables contributors to get on with that which they are best at — producing the work.

Here, at Elfande, we are publishers of creative individuals, Photographers, Illustrators and Designers. We are often asked if we would become agents, but have to decline. Agents are amongst our best customers and, for us to represent anyone would jeapordise our position. To readers of Contact it may often appear that we act as agents because our address details, etc are on some individual's pages. The reason for this is that many people wish to appear in Contact but at the time of production are thinking of moving for one reason or another. Offering the facility to use our details as a contact address enables them to promote their work thus alleviating the possibility of losing potential commissions, as their new details are passed on to enquirers. This is a service which we are happy to provide for our valued customers.

PHOTOGRAPHY BY PETER J MILLARD

This edition of Contact marks the 6th Anniversary of the Contact Annual of Photography and Illustration. The book has grown from 50 pages to well over 700 and I would very much like to think that it has become an essential working tool for those in the communications business. The standard of the work in this current volume is stunning – surely there can't be many visual requirements in the industry which the book couldn't supply?

As in previous editions, you will see work by well-known names, together with the lesser known. The results are often hard to judge. How good was the brief from the Art Director? Did the brief leave much scope for imagination? Did the Account Executive side with the client, or did he do his part in helping push through a lousy concept – but required a stunning result? (and they all want that, don't they?).

Finally, may I express my gratitude to all users of Contact over the last five years, who have been instrumental to the success of the book. However, if you feel there are ways in which the book can still be improved upon then I would like to hear from you, that is, with the exception of the person who keeps asking for a section on aerial photographers – look up NASA! (They are in Cape Canaveral.)

BARRY O'DWYER
Editor

5

Benson & Hedges Gold Awards

The Benson and Hedges Gold Awards is an annual competition for creative work produced in response to a one word brief. In 1989 the word was "Quality", and in 1990 the brief is "Magic".

The Awards invite work from both professional and student photographers, (as well as from illustrators and film/video makers). The work has to be submitted by the last day in June each year.

Professional and student entries are judged separately by a specialist panel, with representatives from the advertising industry, from the media and from the profession. The judges look for creativity and originality, together with a proficient technical ability. Each year three professional photographers, and one student photographer are presented with the top awards, and a further ten highly commended prizes are given across the two categories.

In addition to the prize money awards, all the competition finalists benefit from exposure and publicity, as the award-winning and finalist work from each year's competition creates an exhibition which tours the UK. This is shown first in London, and then visits a further seven venues, ensuring that it is seen by a wide audience.

The photography categories of the Benson and Hedges Gold Awards are organised in conjunction with the Association of Photographers.

For further information, or an entry form write to Benson and Hedges Gold Awards, Welbeck Golin/Harris Communications Ltd, 43 King Street, Covent Garden, London WC2E 8RJ.
Tel: 01-836 6677.

SUE EVANS AND TIM ROBINSON *"THE QUALITIES OF AN ENGLISHMAN"*
Second Professional Photographer in the 1989 Benson and Hedges Gold Awards, received £1,500.

VICTOR DE SCHWANBERG *"BEING THERE"*
First Professional Photographer in the 1989 Benson and Hedges Gold Awards, received a unique gold trophy, and £2,000.

JOHN WHEBLE *"SUMMER DAYS"*
Third Professional Photographer in the 1989 Benson and Hedges
Gold Awards, received £1,000.

MARK GASKIN *"USE/ABUSE"*
First Student Photographer in the 1989 Benson and Hedges Gold
Awards, received a gold medal and £1,000 (the student's
college receives a further £1,000).

Picture this:
The fine art of using copyright

The problem of copyright is one that will not go away. It's a grey, foggy area which most people in the business don't want to acknowledge. If a problem does arise it's one they are only too pleased to pass across to the legal department or solicitor. Turning a blind eye is not the answer, so Contact asked legal experts Stephens Innocent to write this article for anyone who will be commissioning creative work in the coming year.

Stephens Innocent has, for the last seven years, been Britain's only firm of Lawyers specialising in the visual arts.

Formed in 1982 by Mark Stephens and Roslyn Innocent and joined in 1983 by Robin Fry, and in 1985 by Nicola Solomon the firm quickly became known as the leading firm dealing in photography, illustration, painting, sculpture and other creative areas.

The firm has now broadened and can handle a wide range of arts and entertainment matters including fine art, television, film, merchandising, writing and journalism.

The partners are frequent lecturers on copyright at art schools and arts seminars and Robin Fry has contributed to a number of magazines including Image and Creative Review.

Artists and Designers have a rough time; changing briefs, lost artwork, late payment (or on payment) and the vulnerability from being a self employed Artist dealing with a large commercial concern on their standard terms.

Agencies also complain; clueless artists, late delivery and a less than business like sense of urgency in the brief.

Problems with commissions can almost always be traced back to the original arrangements; typically, this is all on the phone but filled out with a tremendous amount of goodwill and the feeling that both sides really know exactly what is needed. The reality of the situation is often different – art directors change, the client decides he wants something a little different (or wants to scrap the whole campaign) and then the illustrator or photographer hears that there is a "problem" on the invoice and that, somehow, the final artwork just doesn't have the "right" feel.

It is absolutely critical, therefore, for both agency and illustrator to establish a clear agreement before any work is carried out . This is a people industry and one often works with personal contacts and it is not unnatural, therefore, that the idea of a full written contract can put the dampeners on what, until then, was a good and positive relationship. Something must be written down, however, since major problems can arise later if the exact terms are not agreed.

A letter outlining the agreed terms ("a confirmation of commission") can be completed by the illustrator and sent to the client once the initial discussions have taken place. As a minimum this should cover the price and format for the finished work, the deadline and what checks or approvals are needed on the preliminary roughs, the exact name of the client (is this the design agency or the ultimate user) and also clear details concerning payment (is this to be on delivery, acceptance or publication?). Art orders sent out by agencies are often just standard printed terms and do not include some of the more important agreed terms. Both the Association of Photographers and the AOI have produced confirmation letters based on the new Copyright, Designs and Patents Act 1988.

One important point which, it seems, is never included is provision for a rejection fee if the work is done but not, for any reason, used.

It is always essential to confirm the exact copyright position; where the client takes an assignment of copyright in the completed work then that person is free to use the image for any purpose even though these may never have been discussed, in advance, with the artist. No additional fee need be paid and no re-use fees can be invoiced to the ultimate client.

The usual position is that the artist is the first owner of the copyright in the completed artwork but that he or she gives permission (a Licence) to the commissioning agency for the use of the artwork for certain specified purposes. Unless there is agreement, in advance, in writing then the copyright will be retained by the artist and will not automatically be owned by the client. It is in the interests of both parties that the exact use is agreed.

Photographers have, to date, been in a different position; until 1989, commissioned photography work has (in the absence of agreement to the contrary) automatically been owned by the commissioner. This has now changed and the Photographer will usually be the first owner of copyright.

One recent case has thrown considerable doubt in this area – an advertising agency, acting on behalf of Gestetner, commissioned an artist to make up some drawings of cats for use in promoting a new product at a trade fair. A fee was agreed and paid on this basis but, later, Gestetner started using the drawings on all their promotional literature and claimed that despite the provisions of the 1956 Copyright Act, they had effective ownership of the copyright.

The High Court did confirm this and stated that the artist had no rights for any further fees even though it was admitted he owned the copyright. The Judge seemed to take the view that if an artist had been paid a very healthy sum of money in order to produce some artwork then it must be right that the commissioner would have all rights relating to that piece. This is, of course, against trade practice and inconsistent with the way creators work in other areas (writers, musicians, playwriters) where fees or royalties are paid depending on the use to which an image or literary work is put rather than the amount of time taken in producing it. Certainly, the AOI, the Association of Photographers and the other creative associations have been voluble in 1989 in restating this basic principle.

Although the established policy of the AOI is that the artwork always remains the property of the illustrator and must be returned after use, there are still certain clients (as opposed to the agencies) who believe that this is not the case and insist that, since they had paid for the work, the artwork must also be owned by them.

Unfortunately, there is no clear established case law confirming that this is the case and, indeed, in another area many professional photographers have had problems in retrieving transparencies or negatives from clients who assumed that, since they had paid for the job, they were entitled to all the materials which they had also paid for.

Whatever one's interpretation of "trade practice", reference to ownership and return of artwork (and transparencies) should be stated in the confirmation of commission and every piece of artwork sent out from the studio must have a clear label on its back giving the name and address and also a statement that the artwork is to be returned to the Artist.

Agencies, artists and designers will all now be aware of the new "Moral Rights" which have been included in the Copyright, Designs and Patent Act 1988 which came into force in August 1989. The new Act gives various rights to the artist in this connection, namely, the right of paternity (i.e. for a credit), the right of integrity (the right to prevent any distortion of the work) and a remedy for false attribution of authorship. There is also a right to privacy but this is limited to photographs of people where these have been commissioned for private and domestic purposes.

The right to a credit is stated to apply to any publication or exhibition of the artwork or when it is included in a film or on television. However, the major exception is that the right does *not* apply in relation to publication in "a newspaper, magazine or similar periodical, or . . . an encyclopaedia, dictionary, year book or other collective work of reference . . . and for the purposes of such publication". Advertising posters, yes – Contact 6, no.000.

The right is, in any case, subject to another difficulty: the right has to be "asserted" and this has to be done by an "instrument in writing signed by the author . . .". Accordingly if the artist wishes to utilise the relevant provisions then, on the back of every piece of artwork which is delivered there should be a statement that the Artist "asserts his right to be identified as author in accordance with Section 77 and 78 Copyright, Designs and Patents Act 1988". The Artist should sign immediately beneath this statement. So much for the bureaucratic process.

However, this major step forward in copyright legislation may be of little effect if the right can be waived by the illustrator. This can be done, by agreeing that the credit should not appear. It would be sad if these new, noble provisions elevating the Artist from a mere workman to a creator should be killed off at birth. I believe that artists and designers should refuse to accept an abandonment of this right unless this is absolutely necessary and clients should recognise that this is so.

Interestingly, in France there is usually a credit for the ad agency; this is in writing and shown at the bottom during the first few seconds of every television advert – it seems that it's not only artists who find the idea of a credit appealing.

The other main moral right which has been brought in by the 1988 Act is a right to "integrity" which is, in fact, stated to be the "right to object to derogatory treatment of work".

This is defined as any "distortion or mutilation of the work or is otherwise prejudicial to the honour or reputation of the author". (It's surprising that Liberte, Egalite and Fraternite are not also included.) The rules are meant to cover any major retouching, mutilation or distortion of the picture. Again, the right does not apply to artwork or photographs made for the purposes of publication in newspapers, magazines or collective works of reference although surprisingly, it will apply to advertising in other media.

I believe that one of the major matters of concern for artists, designers and photographers in the 1990s will be the digital storing of images. This may seem a somewhat obscure point to raise and not relevant but it is, however, extremely important for all creative professionals.

Photographs, pictures and other images are now being converted electronically and stored on computers; data-bases can be built up of these pictures and the images brought up on a Quantel Paintbox or Harry Machine to create new images.

It will be almost impossible to police that storing or manipulation of illustrations or photographs held on these machines but, the economic incentives for clients to create new images in this way are enormous. A client can see a new image being created from a bank of previously commissioned work and can discuss the matter, at the time with the art director and the image can be manipulated exactly to the client's wishes. This will be a much faster and (for the client) more effective way of producing artwork.

Once the pictures have been stored digitially, the copyright position is, unfortunately, somewhat unclear. The 1988 Act brought in (under pressure from Photographers) a specific exception in relation to the use of artistic works to state that the "incidental inclusion of a copyright work in another artistic work will not be an infringement of copyright".

There is some academic argument as to exactly what is meant by "incidental" and whether this means "not deliberate" or whether it simply means a small part of a larger picture. The problem will arise where, if an image is "incidentally" included as part of another picture, then the use may not be a copyright infringement and therefore no royalties or re-use fees need be paid. Whatever the position, no commissioned artwork should be able to be used in this fashion unless the illustrator or photographer has agreed the relevant use fee in advance.

It seems that as soon as a new Copyright Act is brought in, it is almost immediately out of date; my only question is whether we will have to wait another 32 years until the next one.

Robin Fry
Robin Fry is a Senior Partner with media lawyers Stephens Innocent. Further enquiries may be addressed to Nicola Solomon at Stephens Innocent, Columbia House, 69 The Aldwych, London WC2B 4DU, Tel: 01-404 2000, Fax: 01-404 4443.

Cover Story

Feltus puts the F back into Fotography

From sunny Bakersfield to Bog-Bound Duesseldorf through Paris, London, Rome, Moscow and soon Peking "Fritz & Friends" are out to conquer the world. Brain child of US-born, but Europe based Photographer-Designer H. Ross Feltus, these fresh new images hit the European Scene with a sense of relief and excitement.

H. Ross Feltus fell into photography and design the way one falls in love, things just snapped into place when he bought a camera whilst an army medic in Germany. In the beginning he was selling pictures of Heidelberg Castle to tourists and ten years later, we find him running a large photography Design and Graphic Studio in the centre of Duesseldorf, after having worked in many fields of Photography Design and Graphics to worldwide reportage (New York Times, Sunday Times Magazine in London, Stern, etc.) Amongst his first clients were children and adult fashion houses, and he found himself hand in hand with top designers evolving their image and, on occasion, influencing their style. Hence this legendary collaboration with the likes of Ton Sur Ton, Trotinette, Traffic of Delfino and Portobello's the results of which have not only graced shop windows, but also important exhibits in major museums in Europe and even in the Soviet Union. Last spring some was shown at the art directors club in New York. His trade mark is the black and white photo hand coloured with all kinds of collage, graphics, paintings added to create some of the most unique and influential images of our time. Wherever he goes he collects props to use them: popcorn boxes from Paris movie houses, a basket used to carry fish in Southern France, odd bits of furniture people have thrown out. Feltus also shoots colour work for firms such as Sunny, produces posters for the Steif toy company and gives lectures at seminars held by firm manufacturers. And as for the kids in the pictures, sissies and professional models are pushed out of the picture by Ross's own sons and his wild gang of school friends, German, American, Japanese, African, Moroccan, Czech and Israeli. It can get rather strange when Ross is filming and all these countries are represented. Hence his son Fritz inspired his first poster. The result "Fritz the Boxer" has sold 80,000 copies worldwide. Since then the name Fritz & Friends has become a label for photos that bring the world of children closer – a world of acting and dressing up. The themes vary from "Famous" and "Astronauts" to historic persons like "Napoleon and Josephine" and a lot more. When Ross blows the whistle everybody stops fighting, music from Bartok to B.B. King blasts through the studio filled with the wildest of props and the photo happens, miraculously, with Fritz and Friends. Ross Feltus's brainchild, he's decided to exercise his copy right, creating veritable collections of images.

His posters for favoured clients were and are produced in limited editions eagerly snapped up by collectors, but now he has decided to distribute them commercially himself, outside the contract between his studio and the clothing designers as posters, postcards, school stationery and many more graphic applications on clothes and fabrics are making these fabulous images available everywhere.

Further 250 photos out of an image bank of thousands are available in every shape and size, and were recently on view at the National Stationery Fair and the Back to School Show at New York in February 1990. The 1990 H. Ross Feltus Presents Fritz + Friends calendar won several design prizes, including the International Kodak Foto Calendar prize for 1990 and the Forum Design Prize in Hannover, West Germany.

Next Projects – Three Calendars for 1991, various fashion catalogues design + photo and so on.

Beats being a medic I bet! – Ed.

H. Ross Feltus
Kronprinzenstrasse 127
D-4000 Duesseldorf 1
West Germany

European Manifesto

At Photokina in October 1988, at the request of the French organisation, Union des Photographes Createurs, a number of associations representing the interests of advertising and editorial photographers in Europe, met for the first time.

There were many issues of common interest, but the associations were drawn together by their common concern for the many subsequent problems plaguing the image.

Although results of this kind or formal organisation before any real concrete issue can be achieved this group continued to meet at photographic events; SICOB 1989, at the I.I.P. in Arles and most recently at Salon de la Photo, in Paris, where they established a plan of action.

On this last meeting came 'The Manifesto of the Pyramid' a ten point document for presentation to the European Commission. The document calls for the recognition of the rights of photographers – basically the right to be treated with the respect accorded to other authors and creators.

If the 'Pyramid Group' as it has become known wishes to gain the ear of the Commission, then it will be necessary to become a formally recognised body, but first the group must be representative of photographers' interests across Europe.

Currently the following organisations have signed the Manifesto of the Pyramid, they are:
UPC – FRANCE
The Association of Photographers (AFAEP) – GREAT BRITAIN
GUACP – GREECE
BFN – HOLLAND
AFIP – ITALY
FEFPPM & ANIGP – SPAIN
SFF – SWEDEN
DFF – WEST GERMANY

PHOTOGRAPH BY NICK DALY

For more information on the Manifesto of the Pyramid write to
Janet Ibbotson, The Association of Photographers,
9-10 Domingo St., London EC1Y 0TA. UK.

Photographer's Index

Photographer's Index

Photographer's Index

Photographer's Index

★ *John Adams Studios*

156 New Cavendish Street
London W1M 7FJ
England

Tel: 071-636 3408
Fax: 071-436 7131

John Adams, a top ranking
professional known for his
fashion, advertising and
calendar photography, is
constantly exploring new
creative techiques.
He operates on location and
from his fully equipped studio
situated close to the
Telecom Tower.

18

★ *Adams Picture Library*

156 New Cavendish Street
London W1M 7FJ
England

Tel: 071-636 1468
Fax: 071-436 7131

Adams Picture Library is a
general photographic library
stocking many subjects in great
depth. Choose from
approximately half a million
transparencies; the selected
work of over 400
photographers from all over the
world. The library is constantly
being updated with new
material.
Adams Picture Library is
conveniently situated close to
the Telecom Tower.

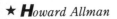

★ **H**oward Allman

Studio 3
40 Bowling Green Lane
London EC1R 0NE
England

Tel: 071-837 0433
Fax: 071-837 7612

Food
Food
Still-life
Food
Food

Home Economy and
Recipe Creation
Ricky Turner 071-482 0473

★ *Peter Anderson*

31A Stansfield Road
London SW9 9RY
England

Tel: 071-737 0851

Specialist areas:
Room sets, interiors and still
life.

Clients include:
Elle Decoration,
Good Housekeeping,
Country Homes and
Interiors,
Homes and Gardens,
Brides, Dorma, Vitsoe UK,
Amtico, Wimpey Homes and
Audioline Telephones.

Reproduction Courtesy of:
Elle Decoration.
Stylist: Claire Lloyd.
Set built by:
Reuben Momrelle.
Set painted by:
Matthew Lauder.

★ **A**nschlag & Goldmann

Heinrich Hertz Str. 13
4280 Borken
Wenden Str. 493
2000 Hamburg 26
West Germany

Tel: 02861 1716-1726
Fax: 02861 64492

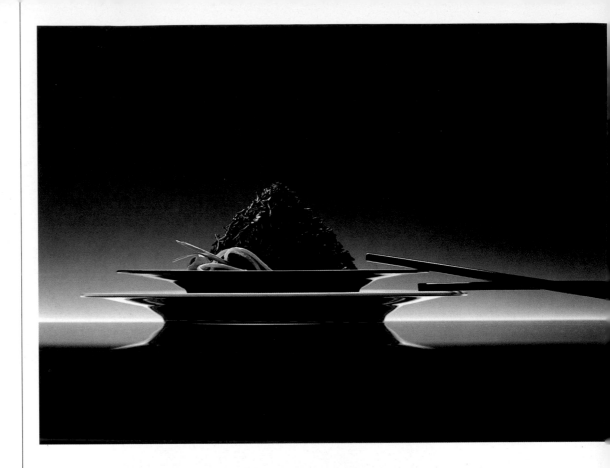

We are specialised food and
people photographers, as
these shots will show you.
A different style, perhaps,
as you are used to, but may
be an interesting alternative
for your clients products.
We can send our portfolio
to you.

★ **M**atthew Antrobus

Unit 406
31 Clerkenwell Close
London EC1R 0AT
England

Tel: 071-251 2837

Specializing in:
Architecture, interiors,
landscapes, industrial,
corporate and location
photography.

Clients include:
London Docklands
Development Corporation,
British Film Institute,
The Architects Journal,
DEGW,
Perkins Engines,
Geiger International,
Michael Manser Associates,
and The Fitzroy Robinson
Partnership.

★ **D**avid Ash

Shaftesbury House
13/14 Hoxton Market
Coronet Street
London N1 6HG
England

Tel: 071-739 0990
Fax: 071-739 9614

Clients include:
Ashridge,
DBD,
Beaujolais Association,
Dixons,
Dolphin,
Ever Ready,
Garden Store,
Hotpoint,
K.P.,
Marks & Spencer,
Mirror Publishing,
Nat West,
Pepsi,
Peter Black,
Portugese Adminstration,
Quantas,
Royal Mail,
Rothchilds,
Sharwoods,
Tesco,
World Coffee Growers,
Wenstrom House.

★ **Zafer Baran**

1 Venn Street
Clapham
London SW4 0AZ
England

Tel: 071-622 9700/627 4225

Abstract and experimental
photography.

This page, top and bottom:
BICC Technologies.

Opposite page:
Wyvern International.

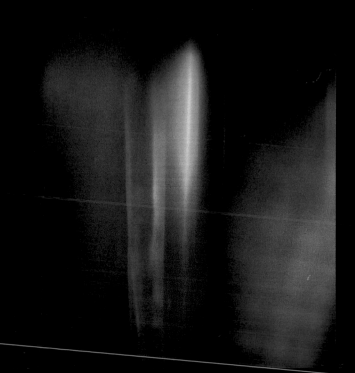

★ **C**olin Barker

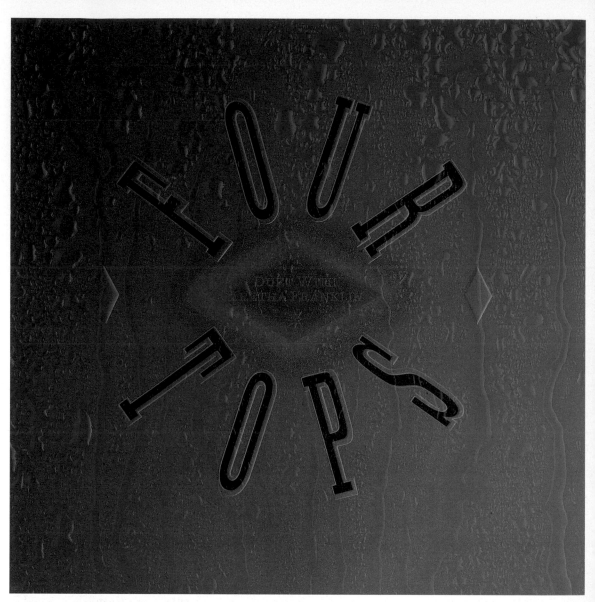

6A Pratt Street
Camden Town
London NW1 0AB
England

Tel: 071-380 1056
Fax: 071-380 0829

Agent:
Francoise Tison
Tel: 071-388 9490
Fax: 071-380 0829

Colin specialises mainly in
'still life', but where
appropriate he prefers to
take out the 'still' aspect by
utilising various in-camera
techniques.

Clients include:
Sony,
Kodak,
National Westminster,
Boots,
Virgin,
House of Fraser,
Crown,
Rimmel,
Mattel,
Revlon,
Motorola and
Prestige.

Top left:
Client: Shoot that Tiger!
Ad: Declan Buckley

Top right:
Client: Sola Sportswear
Models: Rascals

Bottom left:
Client: Nationwide Anglia
Ad: Mike Cavers at
Limbo Limited

Axance
66 Rue Jean-Jacques
Rousseau 75001
Paris

Tel: 40 26 21 26
Fax: 45 08 03 26

Bérénice
Figures Libres Agency
Paris

★ **S**imon *Battensby*

Studio 28
Waterside
44-48 Wharf Road
London N1 7SH
England

Tel: 071-251 4223
Pager: 081-884 3344
Code: Batman

Simon specialises in:
Still life and multiple image
montages which are
produced in camera without
retouching.

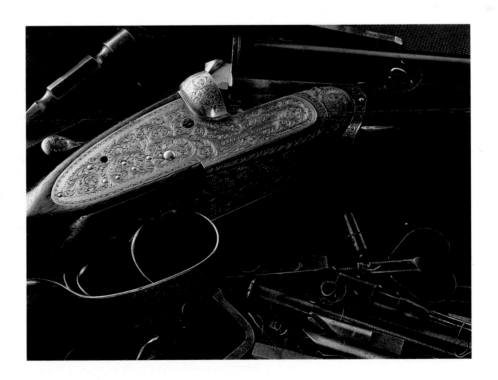

★ *Peter Bailey*

Jan Baldwin

Represents:
Jan Baldwin
Michael Harding
Clint Eley
Grant Symon
Martin Langfield
Miriam Reik
Fiona Pragoff
Lorentz Gullachsen

Agent: Peter Bailey Tel: 071-491 8609/629 5075 Fax: 071-409 2869

Michael Harding

Agent: Peter Bailey Tel: 071-491 8609/629 5075 Fax: 071-409 2869

Agent: Peter Bailey Tel: 071-491 8609/629 5075 Fax: 071-409 2869

Agent: Peter Bailey Tel: 071-491 8609/629 5075 Fax: 071-409 2869

FIONA PRAGOFF

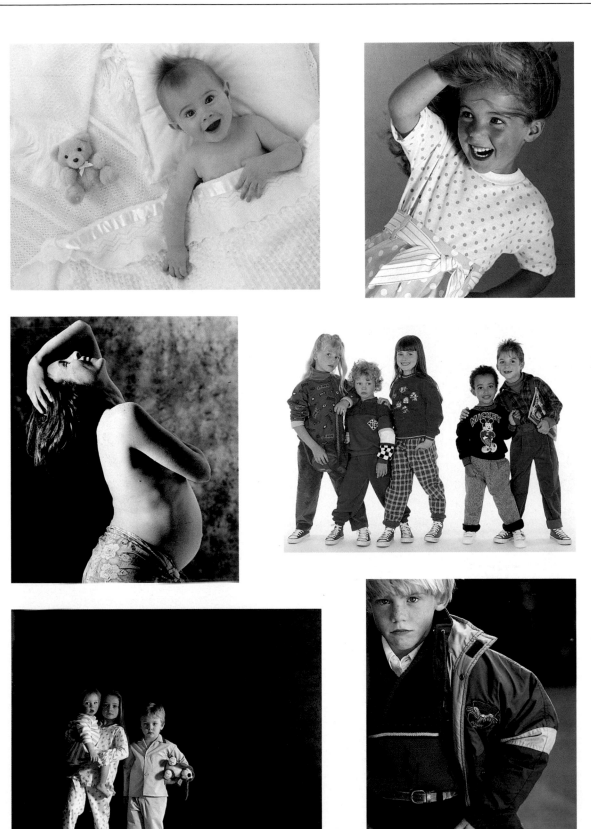

Agent: Peter Bailey Tel: 071-491 8609/629 5075 Fax: 071-409 2869

GULLACHSEN

Agent:
Peter Bailey
Tel: 071-491 8609/6295075
Fax: 071-409 2869

★ *Julian Bajzert*

Margrave Studios
Heathmans Road
London SW6
England

Represented by:
Baz 071-736 6262

★ *P*eter Beavis

Flat 3
100 Brondesbury Villas
London NW6 6AD
England

Tel: 071-624 4884
Pager: 081-884 3344
Callsign: Pete 7

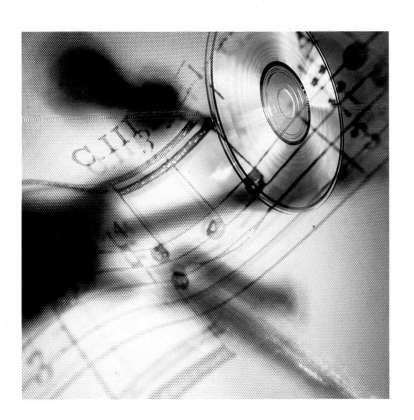

★ *R*on Bambridge

RONBAMBRIDGE
PHOTOGRAPHER

Holborn Studios
Herbal House
10 Back Hill
London EC1
England

Tel: 071-278 4311
Vodaphone 0836 250 965

Ron works in the advertising
and corporate field and also
specializes on panoramic
formats including
360 degrees. He has
received gold and merit
awards at AFAEP for
landscape and people.
Cricket match photograph
opposite page part of a
panoramic calendar that won
best photography at the
National Business Calendar
awards.

Agency: HDM Horner Collis & Kirvan
Client: Peugeot

★ *Michael Banks*

3rd Floor
Colonial Buildings
59-61 Hatton Garden
London EC1N 8LS
England

Tel: 071-430 0769
    071-831 2547 (studio)
Fax: 071-405 3922

I specialise in graphic,
abstract and textural
photography, in the fields of
architecture, product,
location and still-life.
I also have an extensive
abstract photo library
available for use.

Recent clients include:
British Airways,
Thomas Cook, Courtaulds,
Decca, Humber,
McNaughton Paper,
Issey Miyake, R.I.B.A.,
Rosehaugh Stanhope,
Thames Television and
Virgin Records.

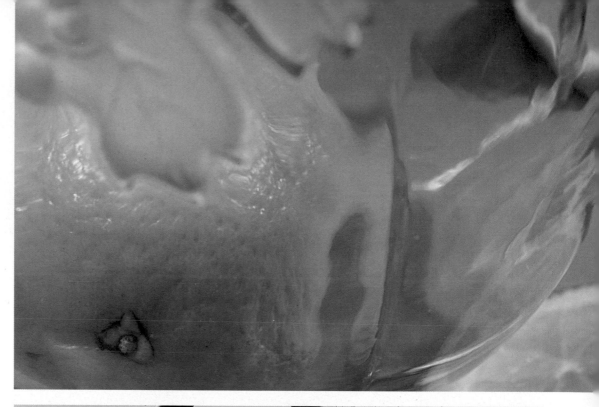

Jean-Pierre Masclet

5 Inverness Mews
London W2 3JK
England

Tel: 071-437 4772
Fax: 071-727 7554

Katy Barker Agency represents:
Bill Batten
Jess Koppel
Lucinda Lambton
Jean-Pierre Masclet
Ken Browar

★ *Matthew J Barlow*

The Workhouse
Photographic Studio
Unit 9
15 Kyrwicks Lane
Birmingham B12 0DE
England

Tel: 021-440 1773
Fax: 021-440 4135

Represented by:
Germaine Walker
Tel: (0527) 31293
Mobile: 0836 594580

★ *Martin Barraud*

32 Great Sutton Street
London EC1V 0DX
England

Tel: 071-253 0732
Fax: 071-253 3104

Agent:
Sue Allatt
Tel: 071-274 8552
Fax: 071-274 8032
Mobile: 0860 224 735

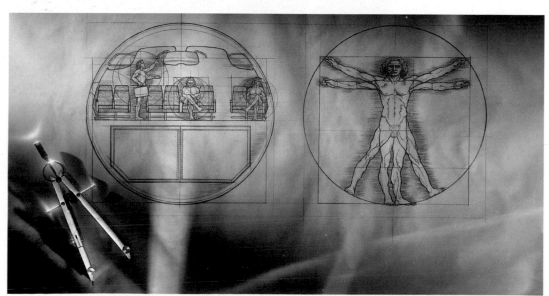

A.D. Alan Docherty

★ **G**reg Bartley

3 Healey Street
Camden
London NW1 8SR
England

Tel: 071-482 4346
Portable: 0831 424 703

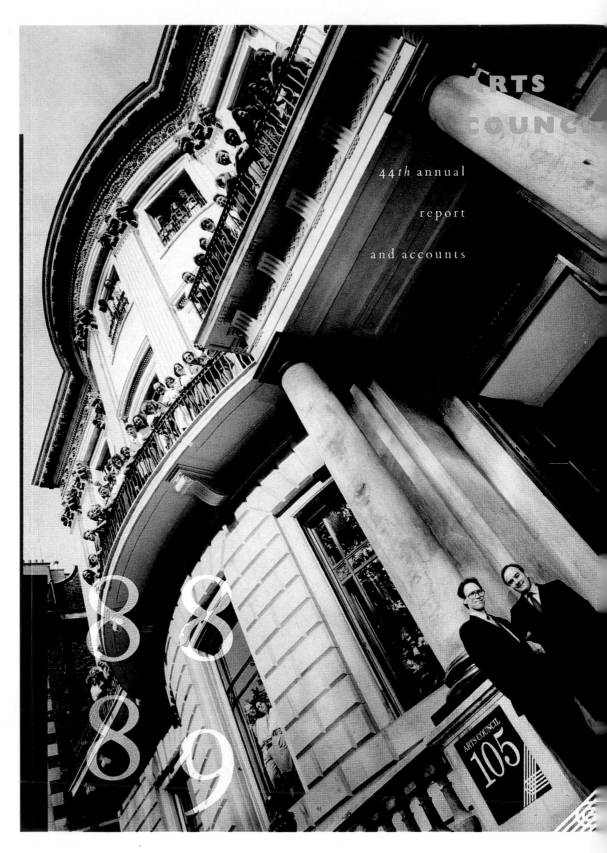

44*th* annual

report

and accounts

Left hand page:
Arts Council Annual Report

Right hand page:
New Electronics Magazine

56 Whitfield Street
London W1P 5RN
England

Tel: 071-637 4786
    071-637 0551

Clients include:
Midland Bank,
British Telecom,
ICL Computers,
Phillips Hi-Fi,
Church's Shoes,
Pioneer Hi-Fi,
Sony

★ **A**ngela Bowskill

14 Moor Street
London W1
England

Tel: 071-407 0261

★ *Barbara Bellingham*

Agent:
Debut Art
28 Navarino Road
London E8 1AD
England

Tel: 071-254 2856
Fax: 071-241 6049

Clients include:
Barclays Bank,
Morgan-Grenfell Laurie,
Spicer-Oppenheim,
3M,
Hilton Hotels,
Sunday Times colour
supplement,
The Observer colour
supplement,
Sunday Telegraph colour
supplement,
Harpers & Queen,
The Radio Times,
The Listener,
Penguin Publishing,
Creative Review.

Commissioned by The Observer colour supplement.

Commissioned by Redwood Publishing.

56

★ *Tony Bown*

35 Adam and Eve Mews
London W8 6UG
England

Tel: 071-938 1967
Fax: 071-937 0039
Mobile: 0836-689064

Entering fascinating,
dedicated optimistic 18th,
glorious year in photography
and still under 35!!*.

* Accurate at time of going
to press.

Broad photographic
experience based on still life.

A constructed image can be taken a long way in the camera

★ *Tony Bown*

Given the light, some subjects stand up for themselves

But sometimes minimum is best

★ *Terrence Beddis*

26-27 Great Sutton Street
London EC1
England

Tel: 071-251 5333
Mobile: 0836 753980
Fax: 071-253 0319

Area of expertise:
Still life

★ *J*ohnny Boylan

6 Mandeville Courtyard
142 Battersea Park Road
London SW11 4NB
England

Tel: 071-622 1214
Fax: 071-720 9656

"Girl with Crow"

Girl: Emma At Power
Make-up: Shiralle Law
Carol Hayes Management
Crow: Battersea Park

★ *J*ohn *David Begg*

Tel: 071-354 2446
(0836) 353339

Architecture
Interiors
Industry
People

Shoralplan Group PL

62

★ **S**teve Bicknell
Productions Ltd

Bicknell

23 Brownlow Mews
London WC1N 2IA
England

Tel: 071-405 1026
Fax: 071-430 2226
Vodafone: 0836 200470

64

★ **S**teve Bisgrove

Red Door Studios
2A, Tabernacle Street
London EC2A 4LU
England

Tel: 071-638 7912
     071-628 3096
Fax: 071-628 3730

Areas of expertise:
Still Life
Landscapes
Architecture
Interiors

★ *P*atrick Blake

8 Chippenham Mews
London W9 2AW
England

Tel: 071-286 5148

These images representing
numbers were all
photographed in our studio
using simple effects
techniques. They are typical
of the work I do for some
clients: marketing property
developments, toys, etc.
I also specialise in still life
and product shots, sets,
interiors, locations and
people.

★ **J**osep Bou

Gran Via 690 Pral 1a
08010 Barcelona
Spain

Tel: 93-232 0243
Fax: 93-300 9038

Specialist in fashion,
beauty and advertising
photography with models.

LOVE FROM WOOLMARK

CRUDO

Mujeres con vida interior

Dior

INDIAN COAST

Pulligan

VODKA ERISTOFF

JIM evolution

Pierre Cardin

DUOMO

Feel Free. Puro sentimiento

W
Warner's

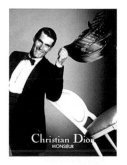

Christian Dior
MONSIEUR

FAINY

BENDEL

ORIOL

★ *Larry Bray*

7 Kensington High Street
London W8 5NP
England

Tel: 071-938 3402
Mobile: 0836 590233
Fax: 0273 439129

Stock represented by:
Telegraph Colour Library
Tel: 071-987 1212

Member of AFAEP.
Location photography for
advertising, corporate, design
and editorial.

Clients worldwide:
American Express,
Barratt,
Boots,
Brent Walker Group,
British Telecom,
Canadian Imperial Bank,
Harrods,
Ministry of Defence,
Pillsbury UK,
Ramada International,
Reed International,
Schlumberger,
T.S.B.,
Unilever,
Woolworth.

★ *Ian Bradshaw*

Represented by
Sandie

2nd Floor
9 Carnaby Street
London W1
England

Tel: 071-287 7177
Mobile: 0836 311339

Area of expertise:
People, location, travel and
corporate identity.

Clients include:
London Docklands, BBC,
Fortune, Readers' Digest,
Hello, Kodak, Pan-Am,
Hill Samuel and ICI.

★ *R*ob Brown

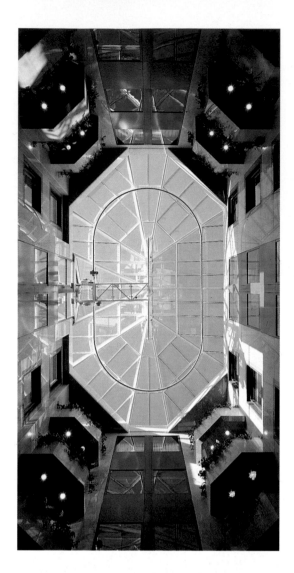

18-22 Barnsbury Street
London N1 1PN
England

Tel: 071-354 3713
Fax: 071-354 3713
Paging: 081-884 3344
Code F3333

Area of expertise:
Architectural, interiors and
people 'In Situ', landscape and
industrial.

Clients include:
Seifert Group,
Broad St Advertising,
Corroll Dempsey Thirkell Ltd,
Zurich Group PLC,
Merivale Moore PLC,
Fitzroy Robinson Partnership,
Benjamin Rowntree Reports,
Shelter.

★ *Richard Brook*

Studio 2
10A Belmont Street
London NW1 8HH
England

Vodaphone 0836 275338

Contact Elfande Art Publishing
Tel: (0737) 242398

Richard photographs people,
people on location,
people in the studio,
people working and
locations without people.
Creative photography, for
advertising and corporate
communications.

★ **D**esmond Burdon

Studio 4
38 St. Oswalds Place
Vauxhall
London SE11 5JE
England

Tel: 071-430 1591
Fax: 071-582 4528

Representatives:
London:
Nicola Crawford
Tel: 071-430 1591
Fax: 071-582 4528

Dusseldorf:
Milena Najdanovic
Tel: 890 3444
Fax 890 3999

Milan:
Vitoria Speziali
Tel: 498 0426
Fax: 481 93788

New York:
Susan Miller
Tel: 905 8400
Fax: 427 7777

Los Angeles:
Bruce Phillips Cohen
Tel: 965 1984
Fax: 965 8623

Top:
Marlboro –
Gold Greenless Trott

Bottom:
British Coal –
Gregory Ellis Martin

★ **D**avid Burch

11 Highbury Terrace Mews
London N5 1UT
England

Tel: 071-359 7435 (office)

Specialising in:
Food and Still Life
Photography.
As well as accepting
commissions, I have an
expanding slide library of
portraits of food containing
hundreds of high quality
transparencies.
These include such things
as raw fruits and vegetables,
breads and pastas, herbs
and spices, coffee beans,
teas and many other
essential foods.

★ *Nick Carman*

32 Great Sutton Street
London EC1V 0DX
England

Tel: 071-253 2863

Agent:
Sandie
Tel: 071-287 7177
Cellphone 0836 311339

Areas of expertise:
Food Specialist

Clients include:
Asda
Sainsbury
Tesco
Marks & Spencer
Nestlé
Landor Associates
Publicis
Mappin & Webb
National Magazines
IPC
Octopus Books

★ *Julian Calder*

2 Alma Studios
32 Stratford Road
Kensington
London W8 6QF
England

Tel: 071-937 3533

Julian Calder has worked on location in 73 countries.

His work has appeared in:
Life
Time
Newsweek
Business
Fortune
Telegraph Magazine
Manager Magazine

Recently he has specialised in company reports:
Allied Lyons
British Oxygen
S & W Berisford
Tate and Lyle
Tiphook
Texaco
Burmah Oil
Whitbread

For B/W, editorial or corporate folios, telephone: 071-937 3533.

Benazir Bhutto, Prime Minister of Pakistan At the Oxford Union

Mirror coating technology, San Francisco BOC Company Report

Andy Goldsworthy's sculpture at the North Pole Life/Independent Magazine.

Harvey's Sherry, Jerez Spain Allied Lyons

★ *Paul Campbell*

1 Alma Studios
32 Stratford Road
London W8 6QF
England

Tel: 071-937 7533

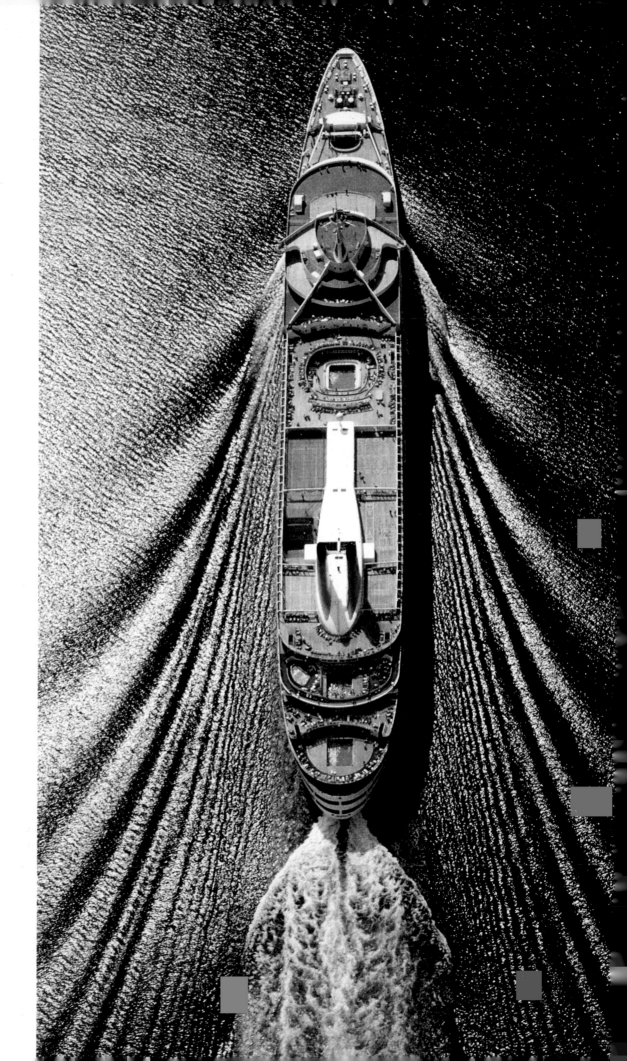

★ *James Cash*
Photographers' Agency

The Glass Mill
1 Battersea Bridge Road
London SW11 3BG
England

Tel: 071-978 5566

Photographers' agent represents:
Alun Crockford
Tim Gummer
Bob Gothard
Alan Newnham
Paul Redman

Alan Newnham   Unit 2, 40-48 Bromells Road, London SW4 0BG   Tel: 071-498 2399

Represented by James Cash   Tel: 071-978 556

Credits: *Client:* Powergen   *Agency:* Michael Peters & Partners   *Art Director:* Chris Lightfoot   Represented by James Cash   Tel: 071-978 5566

Bob Gothard

Paul Redman   31 Springfield Road, London NW8   Tel: 071-624 1630

Represented by James Cash   Tel: 071-978 5566

★ *Simon Cooper*

14 Barkby Road
Queniborough
Leicester LE7 8FD
England

Tel: (0533) 606918/363164

I work in stills with an
emphasis on product,
contemporary interiors and
location photography.
I have also successfully
crossed the divide into
television, working as a
freelance lighting
cameraman, specialising in
arts programmes.
The interchange of
disciplines is invaluable.

★ **M**artin Chaffer

Battersea Park Studios
2 Shuttleworth Road
London SW11 3EA
England

Tel: 071-223 7119
Fax: 071-924 2958

1. – 3.
Client: Fordham Bathrooms
Agency: Three's Company
Art director: Alan Tyers

2.
Client: Dorma
Agency: Trickett and Webb
Art director: Avril Broadley

1.

2.

3.

★ *Jesús M Chamizo*

Calle Pedro Villar, 10
E-28020 Madrid
Spain

Tel: 91-270 87 78

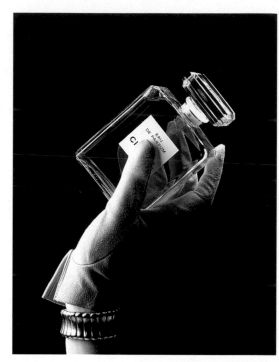

★ Ian Craig

Agent:
Debut Art
28 Navarino Road
London E8 1AD
England

Tel: 071-254 2856
Fax: 071-241 6049

Clients include:
Royal Bank of Scotland,
First Direct Bank,
Nationwide Anglia,
Visa,
Penguin,
Secker and Warburg Publishing,
Phonogram,
The Fred.

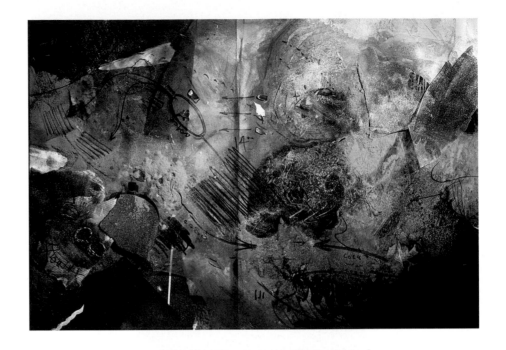

Commissioned by Fitch RS

★ *Richard Cooke*

Tel: (0604) 890556

Represented by:
Derek Harman
1 Rossetti Studios
72 Flood Street
London SW3
England

Tel: 01-352 7635

Alfa Romeo/GGK

★ *Cosmos*

L'ESPACE

Tony Arciero
7 Rue Sentou
92150 Suresnes
France

Tel: 33-1-45061880
Telex: 33-1-40990726

Contact:
Valerie Denis
Christian Marguerie

94

Jean Louis Beaudequin

7 Rue Sentou
92150 Suresnes
France

Tel: 33-1-45061880
Telex: 33-1-40990726

Contact:
Valerie Denis
Christian Marguerie

Le jour où votre Golf vous laissera tomber, **les torts seront sans doute de votre côté.**

Agency: D.D.B. Paris
Art Director: Lucie Pardo

Maurice Smith
7 Rue Sentou
92150 Suresnes
France

Tel: 33-1-45061880
Telex: 33-1-40990726

Contact:
Valerie Denis
Christian Marguerie

Client: Gauloise
Agency: Saatchi and Saatchi
Creative Director:
Pascal Labarazer
Art Director: Laure Merse
Model Maker
Jean Barat
Lizard: Jacana
Art Buyer: Christine Lefers

Hans Hansen
7 Rue Sentou
92150 Suresnes
France

Tel: 33-1-45061880
Telex: 33-1-40990726

Contact:
Valerie Denis
Christian Marguerie

COSMOS
L'ESPACE

Mike Rausch
7 Rue Sentou
92150 Suresnes
France

Tel: 33-1-45061880
Telex: 33-1-40990726

Contact:
Valerie Denis
Christian Marguerie

★ *Cosmos*

Doug Taub
7 Rue Sentou
92150 Suresnes
France

Tel: 33-1-45061880
Fax: 33-1-40990726

Contact:
Valerie Denis
Christian Marguerie

★ *Cosmos*

COSMOS
L'ESPACE

Dominique Dumas
7 Rue Sentou
92150 Suresnes
France

Tel: 33-1-45061880
Telex: 33-1-40990726

Contact:
Valerie Denis
Christian Marguerie

Eric De Cort
7 Rue Sentou
92150 Suresnes
France

Tel: 33-1-45061880
Telex: 33-1-40990726

Contact:
Valerie Denis
Christian Marguerie

Pierre Moreau
7 Rue Sentou
92150 Suresnes
France

Tel: 33-1-45061880
Fax: 33-1-40990726

Contact:
Valerie Denis
Christian Marguerie

Multiple images stripped
together in camera;
with or without size
changes, soft or sharp, opaque
or transparent, (examples:
skies, clouds, rain, fog
shadows, light rays, motion
effect).

Anything your heart desire!!!!

★ Cosmos

L'ESPACE

Christian Occhipinti
7 Rue Sentou
92150 Suresnes
France

Tel: 33-1-45061880
Telex: 33-1-40990726

Contact:
Valerie Denis
Christian Marguerie

ALFA 164. L'ESPRIT ALFA.

Jean Pierre Sandrini
7 Rue Sentou
92150 Suresnes
France

Tel: 33-1-45061880
Telex: 33-1-40990726

Contact:
Valerie Denis
Christian Marguerie

★ *Cosmos*

L'ESPACE

Michel Desmarteau
7 Rue Sentou
92150 Suresnes
France

Tel: 33-1-45061880
Telex: 33-1-40990726

Contact:
Valerie Denis
Christian Marguerie

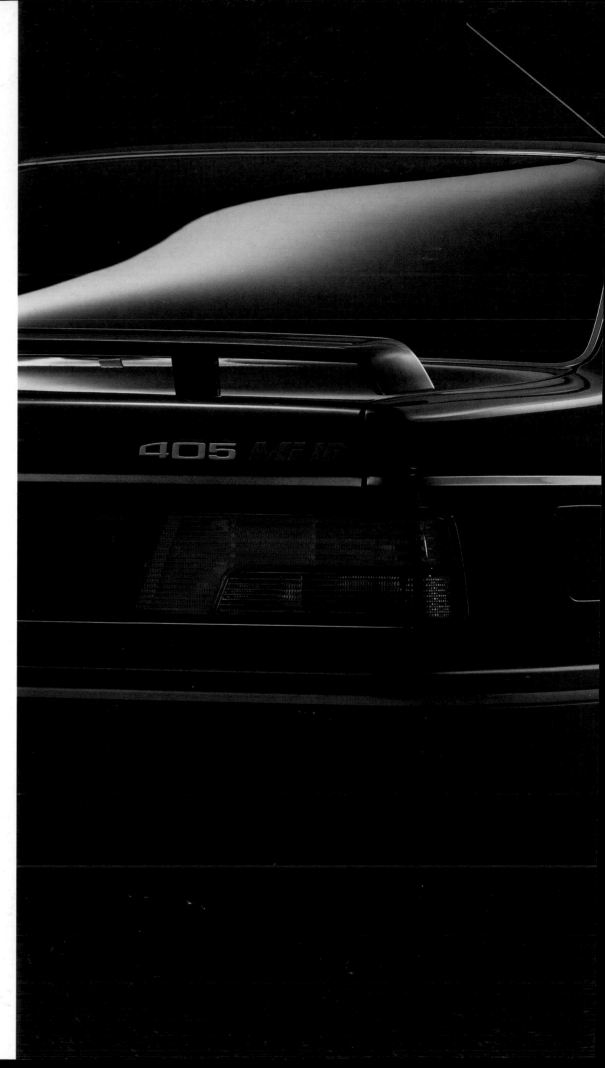

Agency: Ressources
Art Director: P. Rage

Duncan Smith
14A Rosebery Avenue
London EC1R 4TD
England

Tel: 071-837 6873

Agent:
Valerie Denis
Christian Marguerie
7 Rue Sentou
92150 Suresnes
France
Tel: 33-1-45061880
Telex: 33-1-40990726

L'ESPACE

7 Rue Sentou
92150 Suresnes
France

Tel: 33-1-45061880
Telex: 33-1-40990726

Photographers Agent:
Production Photo
Location Studios

★ *Larry Cuffe*

Cuffe Photography
3 Park Quadrant
Glasgow G3 6BS
Scotland

Tel: 041-333 9244

Area of expertise:
Still Life
Food
Drink
Electronics

★ **R**on Davies

22A South Road
Waterloo
Liverpool L22 5PQ
England

Tel: 051-928 7447
Mobile: 0860 434144

Studio based, but works
mostly on location,
in advertising, commercial,
P.R., and travel.
Atmospheric stock shots of
local scenes.

Clients include:
National Museums on
Merseyside, NatWest,
Mecca Leisure,
Merseyside Tourism Board,
Radio City, Royal Life,
Rumbelows and
United Biscuits.

★ **N**ick Daly

12 The Stable Yard
Broomgrove Road
London SW9 3PE
England

Tel: 071-733 1504
Fax: 071-733 1496

Agent Tel: 071-223 2912

Some examples of my recent
work are shown on these two
pages.
To see further examples
please telephone the studio or
Karen on 071-223 2912.

★ *Peter Dazeley*

The Studios
5 Heathmans Road
Parsons Green
London SW6 4TJ
England

Tel: 071-736 3171
Fax: 071-736 3356

My work covers still-life,
cars, fashion, food, people
and corporate literature both
on location and in my large
drive-in studio in Fulham.

Recent clients include:
Amstrad, Audemars Piguet,
Benson and Hedges,
Burton Group, Dunhill, ICL,
Mario Barutti, Mizuno Golf,
Pirelli, Renault, Sony,
Suits You, Stylo Shoes,
Telstar Records,
Volvo and Yonex.

★ *Peter Dazeley*

The Studios
5 Heathmans Road
Parsons Green
London SW6 4TJ
England

Tel: 071-736 3171
Fax: 071-736 3356

★ *Antonia Deutsch*

Central London Studio

Mobile phone:
0836 344 972

Winner of the
Ilford Awards 1989

Lake Titicaca –
printed by Bill Rowlinson.

★ **N***ick Dicks*

The Studio
55 Leroy Street
London SE1 4SN
England

Tel: (Studio) 071-232 1892
Fax: 071-231 4782
Mobile: 0836 345004

Based in London,
Nick specialises in still life and
cars with two fully equipped
studios hc is able to
accomodate large shoots,
with multiple sets.
If you would like to see his tolio
call 071-232 1892.

★ *John Dietrich*

Represented by:
Brian David King
Tel: 021-554 7433
Fax: 021-554 8238

18 West Central Street
London WC1A 1JJ
England

Tel: 071-836 3110
Fax: 071-240 3992

The Gallery
Unit 2
St Oswalds Place
London SE11 5LN
England

Tel: 071-735 8766

Agent:
Damien Birtwistle
Tel: 071-235 4789

Children and fashion
photography.
Studio and location.

★ **N**ick Dolding

28/29 Great Sutton Street
London EC1V 0DS
England

Tel: 071-490 2454

Agent:
Sue Young and Camilla
Tel: 071-262 0189
Fax: 071-262 2160

★ *Julian Easten*

24 The Ivories
Northampton Street
London N1 2HY
England

Tel: 071-241 3679
Fax: 071-704 8107

Advertising and editorial.

Speciality:
Classic large format,
location, landscape, still life.
Toned, tinted and straight
black and white.
Stock shots available.

Top:
Loch Tay for Edge Design.
Client: Cobles.

Bottom:
Product in landscape/hand
tint by Helen 'Z'.

★ **M**ark Evans

3rd Floor
Stonebridge House
16/18 Granby Row
Manchester M1 3PE
England

Tel: (061) 236 5188
Pager: London 081-840 7000
        Outside 0345 333111
Quote pager No. 0346 032
and leave number.

Bardo Fabiani

Tangara Studios
via Revere 8
20100 Milan
Italy

Tel: 010 392 481 8393

Agent:
Chloé Nicholson
Tel: 071-437 0236

FERRÉ

CAPUCCI

VALENTINO

VERSACE

VERSACE

LONDON: CHLOÉ NICHOLSON (01) 437 0236 MILANO: TANGARA PRODUCTIONS S.R.L. (02) 481 8370

30 Upper Gulland Walk
Marquess Estate
London N1 2PF
England

Tel: 071-354 3994

People
Performance
Publishing
Advertising

Clients include:
Methuen,
Collins Publishers,
Seeker & Warburg,
New English Library,
Hodder & Stoughton,
Octopus,
Eavis & Brown,
Benton & Bowles,
British Council,
Performance,
Artsadmin,
British Art Show,
D.I.A.,
STC,
ICA.

Model: Marcella Martinelli

Model: Anna De Freitas

★ *Leonardo Ferrante*

75 Esmond Road
London W4 1JE
England

Tel: 01-994 1203

I specialise in industrial ,
corporate and location
photography.

Clients include:
Sampson Tyrrell,
Wolff Olins and
Smiths Industries.

★ *Graham Finlayson*

Millersbrook House
Woodgreen
Near Fordingbridge
Hampshire SP6 2QX
England

Tel: (0725) 22412
Fax: (0725) 22969

People
Places
Travel

Editorial photography for
leading magazines and, in
similar style, for corporate,
industrial and advertising
clients.

Top:
London auction – *Fortune.*

Centre:
Condemned housing –
known locally, in Liverpool as
'Stalingrad' – *Sports Illustrated.*

Bottom:
Liverpool – *Sports Illustrated.*

★ *Bruce* Fleming

Home: 60 Wimpole Street
        London W1M 7DE
        England
        Tel: 071-486 4001
        Fax: 071-487 3971

Studio: 22 Hesper Mews
        London SW5 0HH
        England
        Tel: 071-370 6028

Biography:
Versatility and flexibility,
backed by 30 years in
advertising and corporate
photography.
I have the know-how,
the total commitment and
the finest equipment to
handle any assignment,
working to exacting
requirements and always
meeting print schedules and
clients deadlines.

Make-up: Martyn Fletcher
Styling: T.J. Productions

My thanks to:

AA
Abbey National
ABI Group
Amari Group
American Express
Anglia Building Society
Arista Records
Austrian Airlines
AW Alloys
BAA
Barclays Bank International
Barratts Group
Batchelor Foods
Bells Whisky
Berger Paints
Berni Inns
Black & Decker
Black & White Whisky
BMW
Boots
Bowery Bank (USA)
British Airways
British American Tobaccos
British Ferries
BP
British Rail
British Steel
Brittania Building Society
Burroughs Computers
Butlins
Camera Effects
Canadian Club
Cannon Insurance
Cariplo Bank (Italy)
Carlsberg
CBS Records
CIBC Canada
Century Asset Mangement
Ceylon Tea
Charterhouse
Chemical Bank (USA)
Chrysler
Cisal (Milan)
COI – Road Safety
Colgate
Colt Ventilation
Cookson Group
CS Investments
Date Logic
Debenhams
EMI – Thorne Group
Enna Insurance (Holland)
Ever Ready
Fairview
Fax 5000
Fernet Branca
Foxboro Group
Grenada Rental
Halifax Building Society
Hamlyn Books
Heineken (Holland)
Heinz
Heron Group

Agency: Midas Direct
Client: Hewlett Packard

★ *Bruce Fleming*

Hertz
Hewlett Packard
Hill Samuel
Holiday Inns International
Honda
Hygena
ICI Group
Israeli Government
Johnsons Marine International
Jones Lang Wootton
JPS – Lotus
Kango-Wolf
Kuwait Bank
Ladbroke Group
Legal & General
Lego
Lever Group
Levi
LHW Futures
Makina
Milk Marketing Board
Mintex
Mitsubishi
Mobil – UK
Modern Alarms
Mortgage Corporation
Nomura Bank
NSPCC
Orient Express MV
Peugeot
Pharmatek
Pheonix Insurance
PPP Medical
Presentation Co.
Prudential Association
Radio Times
Ramada Hotels
Redifussion
Rolex
Royal Air Force
Royal Caribbean Line
Royal Navy
Sainsburys
Sealink
Sekonda
Sony
Sunday Times
Suzuki
Tesco
Thompson Insurance
Trimoco
Triplex Boeing
TSB Bank
Ubix Copiers
Uniroyal
Vendapac
Waterlow
Wistech
Woodhouse Drake & Carey
Woolwich
World Airways
Wrighton
Xyrofin

141

★ *Geoff Fletcher*

Studio Unit G2
Raceview Business Park
Hambridge Road
Newbury
Berkshire RG14 5SA
England

Tel: (0635) 48584
    (0635) 578430 (24 hours)

Industrial
Corporate Advertising
Brochures
Reports

Studio and location, high-tec,
still-life and product shots.

E6 processing available on
premises.

John Pike and Partners,
Architects

Joint European Torus

★ *Jo Foord*

23-28 Penn Street
London N1 5DL
England

Tel: 071-256 0770/80
Fax: 071-739 6543

Area of expertise:
Children and People.

The
Food
Studio

21-22 Great Sutton Street
London EC1V 0DN
England

Tel: 071-253 3085

Food, drink and related
subjects.
Fully equipped modern
kitchen.
To see more examples of
work please contact
Nick Lee on 071-253 3085.

★ **J**im Forrest

82 Chestnut Grove
London SW12 8JJ
England

Tel: 081-673 0936
Mobile: 0836 738841

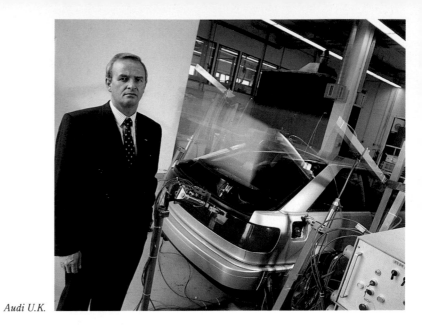

Audi U.K.

Specialising in:
People, cars and a diversity
of location work.

Morgan Cars

January Design

★ *Ian Fraser*

Unit 15/4
Botley Works
Botley
Oxford OX2 0LX
England

Tel: (0865) 250088
Fax: (0865) 791402

Speciality:
Car photography,
Still and Video.
Fully coved studio:
You've seen the ad, now see
the book and the film:
Ring (0865) 250088.

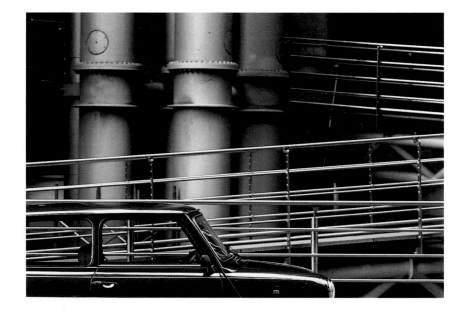

★ *H*. *Ross Feltus*

Photo-Designer BFF, BDG
Kronprinzenstr.   127
D-4000 Düsseldorf 1
Germany

Tel: 0211/306011
Fax: 0211/393398

SPECIAL. EDITION. COMMEMORATIVE. DE. TROTINETTE. 150 YEARS. PHOTOGRAPHY.

Wiener Tangente

Nr. 0233 Angel Machine © H.Ross Feltus -ToN surToN-

H.ROSS FELTUS Photodesigner BFF, BDG
Kronprinzenstr. 127 D-4000 Düsseldorf 1 FRG
Tel: 0211/306011 Fax: 0211/393398

• DANS LES POCHE
• DE NUMÉROS/DE

★ *C*live Frost

25a Rusham Road
London SW12 8TJ
England

Tel: 081-673 6962

Agent: Jo Clark
Tel: 071-404 4006

Kenneth Dixon

Chairman's Statement

★ *Pete Gardner*

5 Charterhouse Works
Eltringham Street
London SW18
England

Tel: 081-871 3975

Still Life
Interiors
Architecture

★ *Stephen J. Garforth*

3A Drayson Mews
London W8 4LY
England

Tel: 071-937 1581
Fax: 071-937 2558

Represented in Madrid by:
Antonio Pastor
La Agencia De Fotografos
Tel: 459 05 56

BMW – AGENCY: BASTON, GREENHILL, ANDREWS

BMW – AGENCY: BASTON, GREENHILL, ANDREWS

ROWNTREE MACKINTOSH – AGENCY: THE SALES MACHINE

'NUTS' – S.J. GARFORTH

★ **P**hilip Gatward

34/37 Bartholomew Close
London EC1 7JN
England

Tel: 071-606 8450
    071-726 4906
Fax: 071-796 4350

Still Life
Modelmaking
Sets
Special effects

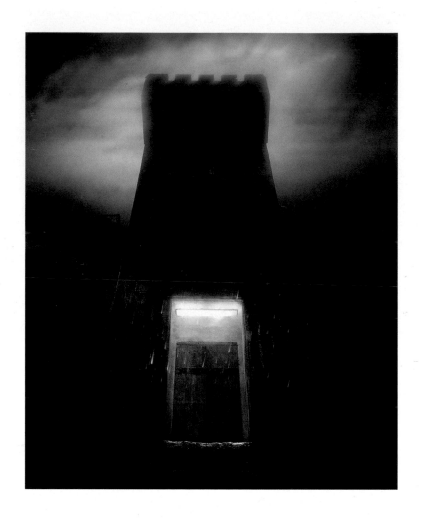

★ **D**avid Gill

73 Leonard Street
London EC2
England

Tel: 071-608 3570

Ineso Studio

Tel: 457-73-97
259-58-83
Fax: 563-49-99

Agent:
Gold-2 S.A.
C/Doctor Fleming
No. 26 Entrep. A
28036 Madrid
Spain

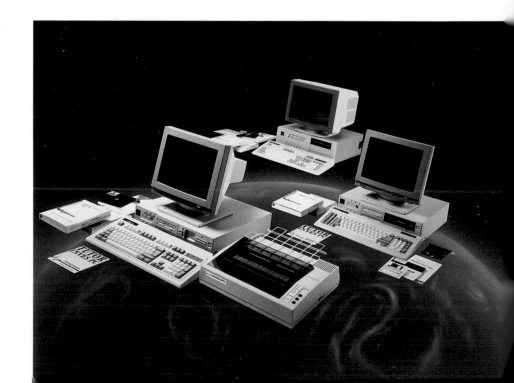

★ *P*hilip Habib

16-20 Underwood Street
London N1 7JQ
England

Tel: 071-253 0824
Fax: 071-250 3833

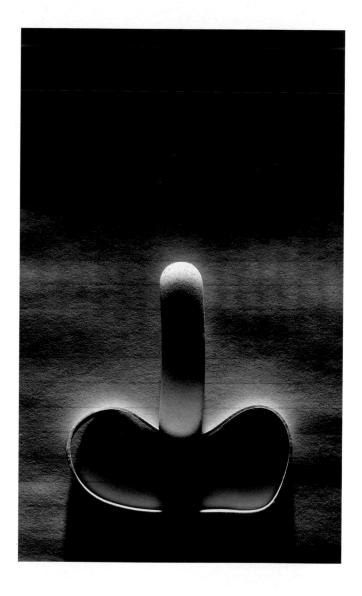

★ *M*ark Hall

6 Monks Drive
London W3 0EQ
England

Tel: 0634 574556
Mobile: 0836 313260

Represented by:
Cherry Ann Wade
Tel: 081-992 4222
Pager: 081-884 3344
Code: Cherry 9

★ **R**alph Hall

2/4 Vestry Street
London N1 7RH
England

Tel: 071-253 0003
Fax: 071-490 1317

People Photographer

★ *Simon Hall*

London based
Tel: 081-673 0162
Fax: 081-675 9036
Mobile: 0831 135300

★ *Graham Henderson*

14 Mandela Street
London NW1 0DU
England

Tel: 071-388 0416
Fax: 071-387 4259

Area of expertise:
Photography and design of
room sets. Locations and
interiors.

Top: Watts Lord Advertising
for Ercol Furniture
Stylist: Annie Waite

Left: Martex Bedlinen
Stylist: Jane Crow

Right: Accross The Line
for Meyer Delbanco

163

★ **M**ark Harwood

Cubitts Yard
James Street
Covent Garden
London WC2E 8PA
England

Tel: 071-836 0832
 081-858 1804
Mobile: 0831 100810

Property in London
is all the better for us.

DEBENHAM
TEWSON &
CHINNOCKS
International Property Advisers

GOVET
STRATEGI
INVESTMENT TRUST P

REPORT AND ACCOU
30th SEPTEMBER 1

Top:
D.T.C. 48 Sheet Poster
Art director: Lorna McDougall
Model Maker: Pipers

Middle:
Govett Annual Report
Art Director: Paul Bayley

Bottom left:
Kango Poster and Brochure
Designer: Adrian Kilby/
Michael Peters

Bottom right:
Bowater Industries Annual
Report
(Mead Show Award Winner)
Designer: Shaun Dew/
The Partners

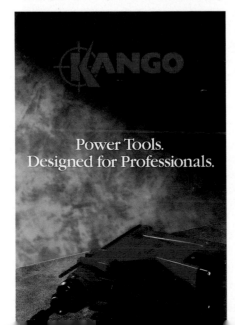

KANGO

Power Tools.
Designed for Professionals.

164

Frank Herholdt

73 Leonard Street
London EC2A 4QS
England

Tel: 071-739 7359
Fax: 071-729 3996

Helicopter:
Client: Grattans
Agency: McCann Erickson
Manchester
Art Director: Chris Forbes
Stylist: Sherry Atkin

Cleopatra:
Client: Colgate
Agency: Publicis Paris
Art Director: Jacques Benoit
Stylist: Zanna Wilford
Setbuilder: Harry Metcalfe

★ *Tim Hill* AFAEP

59 Rosebery Road
Muswell Hill
London N10 2LE
England

Tel: 081-444 0609
Fax: 081-365 3588

Paris agent:
Danny Whittington Eve
Tel: 4241 5454

Area of endeavour:
Large format still life and
food photography for
editorial and design clients.
My unreserved thanks go to
my stylist Zoe and my
assistant Adrian.
Also to my clients, old and
new, who indulge me in
image making.

Stylist:
Zoe Hill 081-444 0609.
Assistant: Adrian Swift.
Processing:
Metro Photographic
*Shoes for Miss Faversham's
bedroom:*
Emma Hope 071-833 2367.
*'The Huntsman's Lodge'
courtesy of:*
Pinneys of Scotland and
The Design Solution.
Christmas wreath by:
Paula Pryke Flowers
071-837 7336.

★ **P**eter Hince

PETER HINCE
01 729 6727

Shaftesbury House
13/14 Hoxton Market
Coronet Street
London N1 6HG
England

Tel: 071-729 6727
Fax: 071-739 2321
Mobile: 0860 326975

Paris
Represented by Cosmos
7 Rue Sentou
92150 Suresnes
Tel: 33 (1) 45 06 18 80
Fax: 33 (1) 40 99 07 26
Contact: Valérie Denis

People, Fashion and Beauty.
In the studio, on location, in
settings and situations.
For a wide variety of
agencies, design groups and
publishers.

Clients include:
Barclaycard,
Boots,
BMW,
CBS,
Channel 4 TV,
Clark Jeans,
Dolcis,
Dunlop/Slazenger,
Gillette,
Harp Lager,
House of Fraser,
Ralph Lauren,
Prudential Insurance,
Titleist Golf Wear,
Wella,
Wolsey
World Wildlife Fund.

★ **A**drian Hobbs

18-20 St John's Street
London EC1
England

Tel: 071-251 9441

★ **I**an Hooton

Conran Studios
29/31 Brewery Road
London N7 9QN
England

Tel: 071-607 5386

Contact: Ian Hooton

Clients include: T.S.B. Bank,
Alberto VO5, L'Oreal,
Virgin, Saatchi & Saatchi,
Ilford Films, Wella,
Schwarzkopf, Just 17,
Woman Magazine, Prima,
Bella, Womens Realm,
Women & Home, Essentials,
More Magazine and
Woman's Own.

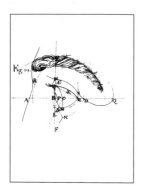

Alexandra Studios
3 Jubilee Place
London SW3 3TD
England

Tel: 071-352 3649
Fax: 071-352 3669

Agent:
Sue Young & Camilla
Partnership
Tel: 071-262 0189

Clients include:
Ford,
Wrangler,
Conran Advertising,
Bass,
Bang & Olofsan,
Federal Express,
Epson Computers,
Island Records,
Atlantic Records N.Y. and
Alliance & Leicester.

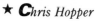
★ *Chris Hopper*

60 St Stephens Gardens
London W2 5NJ
England

Tel: 071-221 1621
Mobile: 0831 449582

Areas of speciality:
Still Life
People
(Corporate brochures and
annual reports).

Top:
Courtesy of Harrison Drape.

Lower:
Courtesy of
Equity & Law PLC.

★ *Tony Hutchings*

44 Earlham Street
Covent Garden
London WC2H 9LA
England

Tel: 071-379 6397

Agent: Sylvia Schroer
Tel: 071-326 4917

Clients include:
Advertising agencies, book
publishers, design studios
and magazine publishers
and subjects are 'still life',
concept ideas, products and
themes, etc.

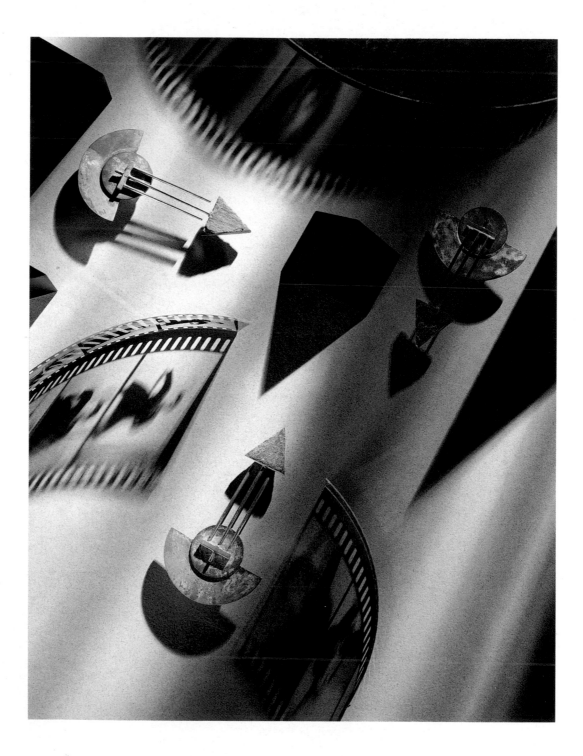

★ *C*hris Bell

Studio 1
275 Kensal Road
North Kensington
London W10 5DB
England

Tel: 081-969 3119
Fax: 081-960 0423

For imaginative location
shots and studio still-life,
which does not always have
to be still, give me a ring.

★ **C***hris Honeywell*

33 Marston Street
Oxford OX4 1JU
England

Tel: (0865) 246311
    (0865) 793278 (Studio)
Message Pager: 0399 1133
Pager no. 740237

Specialising in:
Corporate and Industrial
Photography at home and
abroad.

Client:
The Item Group (06286-62517).
For cover of British Telecom
Internal Magazine 'Prospect'.

★ *Michael Jones*

Flat 2
4 Cromwell Road
Teddington
Middlesex TW11 9EH
England

Tel: 081-977 4064

Architecture, interiors and
landscape.

★ *T*im *Imrie*

34 North Rise
St Georges Fields
Albion Street
London W2 2YB
England

Tel: 071-402 7517

Agent:
Anna Tait
Tel: 071-402 7517

High profile clients.
Photography for design
groups, quality magazines
and book publishers.
Recently moved to spacious
studio in Kensington with
brand new kitchen and set
building facilities.
Location photography
UK and abroad.

Client this page:
Trusthouse Forte

85 Stanthorpe Road
London SW16 2EA
England

Tel: 081-677 4412
Fax: 081-769 3046

Represents:
Michael Crockett
Eitan Lee Al
Brian Leonard
Steve Lyne
Owen Smith

EITAN LEE AL

REPRESENTED BY ELIZABETH JAMES 081-677 4412

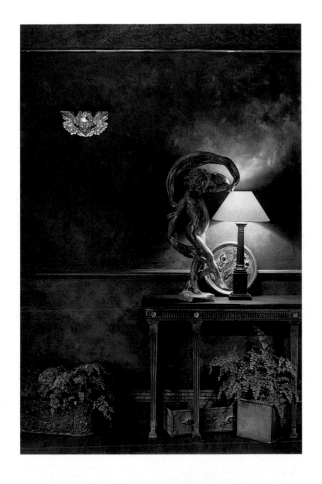

★ **D**avid Kampfner

Southern Light Studios
35A Britannia Row
London N1 8QH
England

Tel: 071-359 3605
Fax: 071-359 1454
Vodafone: 0836 231347

Paris: 1 42 66 05 05
Frankfurt: 69-298 0070

Specialising in:
People
Locations

Client list:
Abbey National,
Barclays Bank,
Channel 4 Television,
Courage,
Crown Berger,
The Home Office,
Premier Brands,
Vauxhall Opel,
The Guardian,
The Independent,
The Sunday Telegraph.

★ *D*avid Kelly

Cassidy Road
London SW6 5QH
England

Tel: 071-736 6205/7694

★ *Paul Kemp*

REPRESENTED BY

HORTON STEPHENS

Agent:
Horton Stephens
Tel: 071-485 2082
Fax: 071-267 7590

Paul Kemp
stills showreel
available outside
United Kingdom.

★ *Robin Kiashek*

REPRESENTED BY

**HORTON
STEPHENS**

Agent:
Horton Stephens
Tel: 071-485 2082
Fax: 071-267 7590

★ *Howard Kingsnorth*

27-31 Earl Street
London EC2A 2AL
England

Tel: 071-247 4765
Fax: 071-247 4836
Mobile: 0860 418 378

For Reel:
Contact Cassar Films
Tel: 071-434 2841

Clients include:
BA
BAe
Currie Motors
Digital
Jeyes
JVC
Marriott
Philips
Post Office
Toyota
UDT
Vauxhall

Advertising:
Stills & Motion

14a Rosebery Avenue
London EC1 4TD
England

Tel: 071-837 6395
    071-833 0510

Recent clients include:
Marks and Spencer,
Birds Eye, Sharwoods,
Brooke Bond, Asda,
Safeway, Unilever,
Ross and Young Foods,
Cadbury, Baxters, Lyons,
Walls, Heinz, Time Life,
Milk Marketing Board,
British Meat,
British Telecom, Courage,
Guiness, RHM, Tesco,
Virgin Airways and
British Airways.

★ *Jess Koppel*

65/69 Leonard Street
London EC2
England

Tel: 071-739 6642

Agent:
Katy Barker
Tel: 071-437 4772
Fax: 071-727 7554

★ *John Knill*

6 Hesper Mews
London SW5 0HH
England

Tel: 071-373 4896
Fax: 071-244 6091

Area of expertise:
Still Life.
Food.
Drink.
People.

★ **B**ob Komar

6 Mandeville Courtyard
142 Battersea Park Road
London SW11 4NB
England

Tel: 071-622 3242
Fax: 071-720 9656

Agent: Chloé Nicholson
Tel: 071-437 0236

★ **S**teve Lee

1 Rosoman Place
London EC1R 0YJ
England

Tel: 071-837 5204
Fax: 071-278 2507

Area of expertise:
Food and Still Life.
Location work undertaken.

The Studio consists of a fully
equipped modern kitchen
and props area.

'Ready Meals' Courtesy of
Peter Day, Design Studio,
Sainsburys PLC.

The Tea Warehouse
10A Lant Street
London SE1 1QA
England

Tel: 071-378 7544
Fax: 071-378 1867

Paris agent:
Valerie Denis at Cosmos
Tel: 331 45061880

Top far left/middle far left:
Ad Basil Christiansen
CW: Damon O'Leary.
For *'Elements of Creda
Campaign'.*

★ *George Logan*

50A Rosebery Avenue
London EC1
England

Tel: 071-833 0799/8189

Agent:
Noelle Pickford
Tel: 071-584 0908

Golf Ball for Spalding.
Art director: Joy Vaughn at
Billington Jackson.

Paper Car for Texaco.
Art director: Roy Macaloney
at D.M.B. & B.

Chair for Virgin Altantic.
Art director: John Jessup at
W.M.G.O.

★ *Derek Lomas*

69 Lambeth Walk
London SE11 1DX
England

Tel: 071-735 0993

Clients include:
Conde Nast, G.Q.,
Good Housekeeping,
Marie Claire,
Michael Peters Group,
Options and
Womans Journal.

Represented by:
Susan Griggs Agency
17 Victoria Grove
London W8 5RW
England

Tel: 071-584 6738
(Studio) 071-727 7488
Fax: 071-584 1732

Children, fashion, health and
beauty, portraits and crafts.

Clients include:
Birthright,
Brides,
Coley Porter Bell,
Conran Mothercare,
Country Living,
Cow & Gate,
Ebury Books,
Elle,
Good Housekeeping,
Great Ormond Street Hospital,
Image,
JWT,
Laura Ashley,
LLE+H,
Marie Claire,
Next,
Options,
Small Advertising
Vogue.

Top:
Cow & Gate

Bottom:
London Portrait

★ *Anna Loscher*

Juan Ramón Jiménez, 22
28036 Madrid
Spain

Tel: 010 341 259 9015

Member of the Madrid
Association of Advertising
and Fashion Photographers.
German, studio in Madrid
since 1979.
Specialization in B/W,
Still life and portrait.
Works mainly for magazines
and editing houses in Spain,
Germany and Switzerland.
Also advertising
photography.

★ **B**ill Lyons *Photography*

P.O. Box 2089
Amman
Jordan

Tel: 962 6 641 559
Fax: 962 6 646 229

Corporate and editorial
assignments undertaken
throughout the Middle East

Clients include:
American Express
Asea Brown Boveri
Cable & Wireless
Euromoney Magazine
Le Figaro Magazine
Life
National Geographic
Newsweek
Pepsico
Racal
Stern
Sulzer
Sunday Times
Thomson CSF
Time

Samples on request.

★ **A**lan Marsh

2nd Floor
11, Lever Street
London EC1V 3QU
England

Tel: 071-490 0952

Represented by:
Lucia Wilson
Tel: 081-209 1867

Areas of expertise:
Still-Life/Food.

Nadia Mackenzie

Studio 005
Canalot Studios
222 Kensal Road
London W10 5BN
England

Tel: 081-964 0672
       071-402 7215

Areas of expertise:
Nadia works on location
specialishing in interiors,
people and places.

Client: Elle Decoration

★ **B**ob Marchant

Stanley House
St Chad's Place
London WC1X 9HH
England

Tel: 071-278 6829
Fax: 071-278 1554
Mobile: 0836 739231

Bob also directs commercials
Please 'phone for showreel.

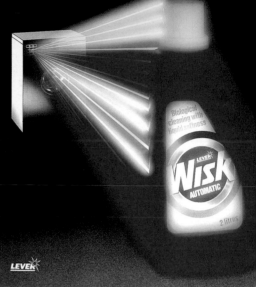

★ *Dick Marsh*

Represented by:
Mary MacKillop
16 Norfolk Mansions
Prince of Wales Drive
London SW11 4HL
England

Tel: 071-622 4111

Area of expertise:
Still Life

Clients include:
Garrards,
Castrol,
Kodak,
Cutty Sark,
Sun Life,
Hambros,
National Westminster Bank,
Financial Times,
Rolex,
Dunhill
Burburys
Armitage Shanks
The Suite Co
Birds Eye
RAF

★ *Jiven Marvaha*

26 Cheltenham Close
New Malden
Surrey KT3 3EY
England

Tel: 081-942 8148
Mobile: 0860 594929

McKechnie & McGee
('Phileas Fogg' snacks) for
'Marketing' Magazine.

Daton Systems.
For Daton and
Flying-Pig Design.

★ **P**hil *Mastores*

47 Sandringham Road
London NW2 5EP
England

Tel: 081-451 5985

Area of expertise:
Architecture
Interiors
Landscape

Clients include:
Addison Design Ltd,
BDP,
Elsom Pack & Roberts
Partnership,
GRE Properties,
The Hammond Design
Partnership,
Scott Brownrigg & Turner,
Sheppard Robson & Partners,
Skidmore Owings & Merrill,
Thorn EMI,
Vitra Ltd.

Gallaher Ltd
Building Design Partnership

Sun Life of Canada
Elsom Pack & Roberts Partnership

★ **M**atthew May

Free Eye Studios
64 Rochester Place
London NW1 9JX
England

Tel: 071-267 8827/37
Fax: 071-482 2340
Mobile: 0836 354787

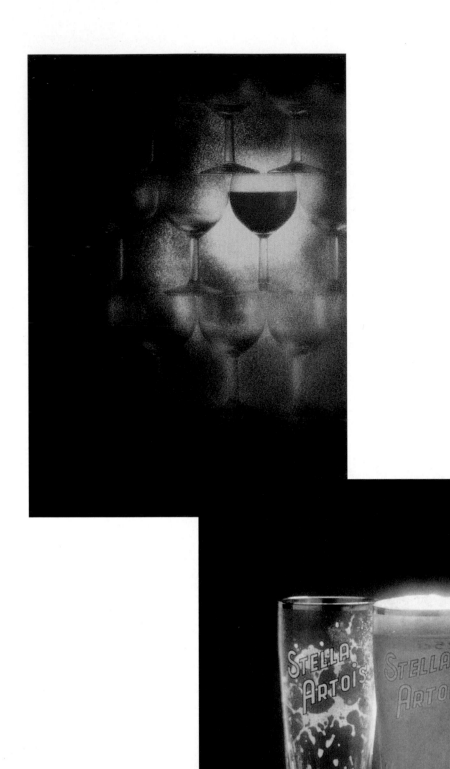

★ *A*nthony Marsland

Beechwood Studio
6-8 Vestry Street
London N1 7RE
England

Tel: 071-490 4177
Fax: 071-253 3923

Agent:
Jonathan Marsland
1 Little Argyll Street
London W1R 5DB
Tel: 071-734 0734
Fax: 071-734 0663
Mobile: 0836 372701

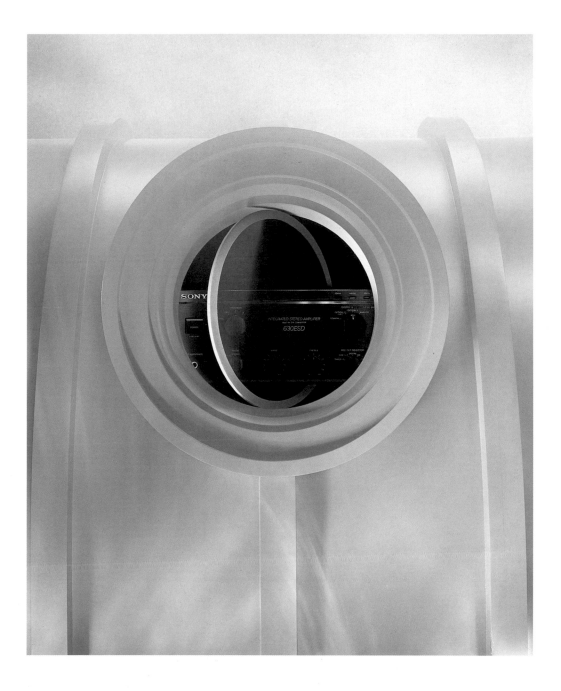

★ **B**arry Meekums

1 Marylebone Mews
London W1M 7LF
England

Tel: 071-487 5233

Agent:
Noelle Pickford
Tel: 071-584 0908

★ **T***revor Melton*

13 Heliport Estate
40 Lombard Road
London SW11 3RE
England

Tel: 071-223 6892
Fax: 071-223 7098

Art director: Mark Beale.
Client: Kahlua/J.R. Phillips.
Agency: PurchasePoint
Group Ltd.

★ *P*eter *J Millard*

Based in London,
but has camera, will travel.

Tel: 071-381 1038
Mobile: 0831 465240

←

For best results,
turn this page through
90 degrees
clockwise.
←

★ *Neill Menneer*

1 Argyle Street
Bath
Avon BA2 4BA
England

Tel: (0225) 460063

Agent:
Debut Art
28 Navarino Road
London E8 1AD
Tel: 071-254 2856
Fax: 071-241 6049

Specialises in corporate location work.

Clients include:
Coutts & Co,
Midland Bank,
BAT Industries,
Rank Xerox,
TSB,
Coopers and Lybrand,
CNA Reinsurance,
Royal Caribbean,
Novotel,
Rugby Securities,
Sunday Times colour
supplement,
Sunday Telegraph colour
supplement,
The Observer colour
supplement,
Harpers and Queen,
Elle,
Company,
Country Homes and Interiors.

Commissioned by CNA Reinsurance.

Commissioned by Dorlands for BAT Industries.

Commissioned by D4 Design for Coutts & Co.

Commissioned by Coopers and Lybrand.

★ **C**olin Mills

23-28 Penn Street
London N1 5DL
England

Tel: 071-739 7694
Fax: 071-739 6543

Agent:
Jenny Ungless
14, Oakhill Road
London SW15 2QU
Tel: 081-870 7916

Area of expertise:
Still Life, Roomsets,
Special Effects.

Clients include:
British Telecom,
Heuga International,
House of Fraser,
Rank Xerox,
Bentalls,
IBM,
Philips.

★ *R*ay Moller

West Point
36/37 Warple Way
London W3 0RX
England

Tel: 081-743 7679

Agent:
Geoff Elliott
Tel: 071-430 2466

Picture reproduced courtesy of:
Roman Yarns Knitwear Design
– Annabel Fox.

Hair and make-up:
Lisa Collard

★ *Ivar Mjell*

Kloster Port 4A
DK/8000
Arhus C
Denmark

Tel: 010 4586 191674

Camaflage Studios
The Basement
D' Warehouse
Metropolitan Wharf
Wapping Wall
London E1 9SS
England

Tel: 071-481 9114
Fax: 071-480 7683

Areas of expertise:
Fashion
Beauty and
Still Life for Advertising
Design
Publishing
and P.R.

Clients include:
Camel International
Aitch Group PLC
Ice Jeans
Gallini
Island Records
Virgin Records
Polydor
E.G. Music
Mullard Electronics
Review Clothing
G.B. Clothing
Various Advertising Agencies

★ **A**drian Mott Photography

Mill House
Chapel Place
Rivington Street
London EC2A 3DQ
England

Tel: 071-729 5910
Fax: 071-729 2386

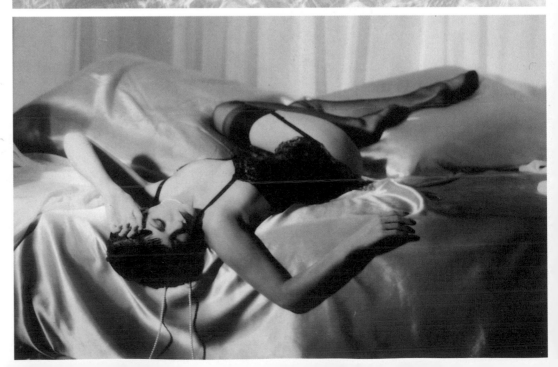

★ **T**im *Motion*

91 St Marks Road
London W10 6JS
England

Tel: 081-960 6102

Experienced in location,
travel, architecture and
aerial photography, portraits
and interiors, for advertising,
annual reports and
brochures.

Clients include:
Kuwait Airways,
Berisford International,
Dominion International,
National Data Corporation,
PPP,
Woolworths,
Barbados Tourist Board,
Indonesian Tourist Board,
Magazines and Newspapers.

Stock library of Jazz and
Blues artistes.

Speaks French, Portuguese
and Spanish.

Bottom:
Art Blakey

★ *J*ohn *Moss*

6 Queen's Terrace
Windsor
Berkshire SL4 2AR
England

Tel: (0753) 865440

Area of expertise:
Annual reports, brochures,
people, industry, travel and
location.

Clients include:
Mobil, Exxon,
Schlumberger, Pepsi-Cola,
Rank Xerox, Digital,
American and Japanese
Banks.

★ *Julian Nieman*

Represented by:
Susan Griggs Agency
17 Victoria Grove
London W8 5RW
England

Tel: 071-584 6738
Fax: 071-584 1732

Studio and location,
architecture, industry,
hotels and restaurants,
landscapes, corporate
portraits, children,
still lives and food.

Clients include:
Astle Horman,
CBS,
Conran Design,
Country Life,
Creative Direction,
European Travel & Life,
Marriott Hotels,
Mothercare,
Readers Digest,
Smithsonian,
Thames Water,
Travel Holiday
Travel & Leisure.

1. *Self.*

2.
Travel & Leisure.

Mothercare.
3.

★ *Greg O'Shea*

GREG ● SHEA

The Worx
45 Balfe Street
London N1 9EF
England

Tel: 071-833 0199
Pager: 081-884 3344
I.D.: F1590

Speciality:
People in Location.

Hewlett Packard

British Telecom

6 Lingwood Walk
Bassett
Southampton
SO1 7GL
England

Tel: 0703 768218

For Agent's phone and fax
numbers in London, contact
above.

Dominic, Medway College
of Design graduate,
photographs people from all
walks of life for a variety of
clients. He shoots on
locations, in their chosen
environment or in front of a
simple backdrop. His
colour/mono portfolio
speaks for itself.

Marquess of Bath,
Longleat House

★ *A*ndrew Olney

32 Great Sutton Street
London EC1V 0DX
England

Fax: 071-253 3104

Agent:
Andrea Rosenberg
Tel: 081-746 0694

★ **B**rian *Phipps*

Peregrine House
Enborne Street
Newbury
Berkshire RG14 6RP
England

Tel: (0635) 42585
Fax: (0635) 528775
Mobile: (0836) 289377

I don't work with agents.

Write or 'phone me direct
and I'll send you a minifolio
then if you're interested in
seeing more I'll bring you a
portfolio and discuss your
next project.

Photography – no reps, no
excuses and no inflated
prices.

B.M.W. – Backdrop by Nick Walton

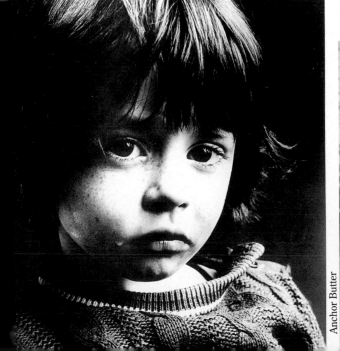

★ **Erik Pelham** A.M.P.A.

79 Wilding Road
Wallingford
Oxon OX10 8AH
England

Tel: (0491) 33568

Represented by:
Philip Millington-Hawes

Working with an
experienced assistant,
Erik specialises in lighting
photography for a wide
range of clients for:
brochures, advertising,
book publishing and
PR photography.

Clients include:
National Trust, Longmans,
Hodder & Stoughton,
Design in Action,
Vernon Oakley Design,
House & Garden and
Eurobook.

*Arrangement, production and
assistance by:*
Philip Millington-Hawes

★ *R*od Panichelli

60A Bramble Walk
Epsom, Surrey
KT18 7TB
England

Tel: (03727) 26950

Agent required U.K. based
to organize commissions.

Scenic locations featuring
World and U.K. Travel for
advertising and editorial.

Clients include:
British West Indian Airways,
Summerfield Morgenthau –
MD&A,   Fuji Film Japan,
British Airways Holidays,
Bartle Bogle Hegarty,
Octopus Publishing,
The Sunday Times,
Carlton Luggage.

Stock syndication
London-Milan-Tokyo

239

★ *T*im Platt

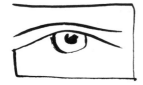

12A Peacock Yard
Kennington
London SE17 3LH
England

Tel: 071-703 2779
Fax: 071-701 0026

Specialising in:
Advertising
Design
Music
Editorial

A SHOT OF SHERRY

by
Emma Hope

CROFT PARTICULAR : PALER BY DESIGN

★ *G*raham *Precey*

Basement
Kingsley House
Avonmore Place
London W14 8RY
England

Agent: Courtney Hildyard

Tel: 071-603 2690
Fax: 071-602 8616

Food & Still life.

★ *David Preutz*

Middlesex House
34-42 Cleveland Street
London W1
England

Tel: 071-636 7072

Some recent clients include:
American Express
Lloyds Bank
Barclaycard
Gonzalez Byass
ICI
Jose Cuervo
Tuborg
Imperial Tobaccos
Yashica and
The Occasional Animal

★ *Ed Pritchard*

144 Shaftesbury Avenue
Covent Garden
London WC2H 8HL
England

Tel: 071-836 0512
        071-839 1613
Fax: 071-839 7509
Mobile: 0836 289 350

Houses of Parliament
Lloyd's of London
Big Ben

Houses of Parliament
Lloyd's of London
Big Ben

★ *John Quinn*

26D Haugh Lane
Hexham
Northumberland NE46 3PU
England

Tel: (0434) 606822
Fax: (0434) 608263
Car: 0860 543548

Agent: Courtney Hildyard
Tel: 071-837 8783

Can order a coffee, beer,
wine (Red, White or Rose)
and ask for the toilet, in
French, Spanish,
Portuguese, German, Italian,
American, Australian and
English.

Can also shoot pictures in
French, Spanish,
Portuguese, German, Italian,
American . . . .

★ *Derek Richards*

1 Alma Studios
32, Stratford Road
London W8 6QF
England

Tel: 071-937 7533
Fax: 071-937 8285

Agent:
Noelle Pickford
Tel: 071-584 0908

Specializing in: people,
travel, locations, corporate
reports for Ad. Agencies and
Design Groups.

Above picture:
A/D: Dick Poole
Agency: JWT
Client: Teachers Whisky

★ **B**ill Richmond

BMR Studios
51-55 Stirling Road
Chiswick Park
London W3 8DJ
England

Tel: 081-993 9641
      081-993 5545
Fax: 081-993 7589
Portable: 0836 674730

Expertise:
Still Life
Food
Roomsets
Interiors
Special Effects
(inc Front Projection)

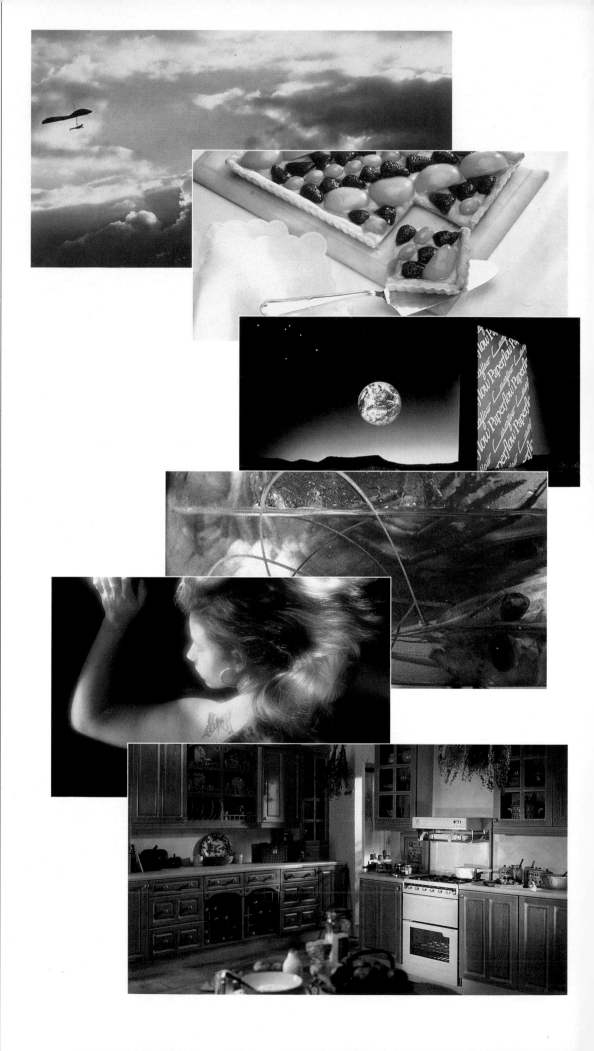

★ **R**ichard *Fotógrafos*

Canaán
Número Cuatro
Bajos – 08023
Barcelona
Spain

Tel: 4189995/4187719

Richards Photographs:
Our work covers advertising
and fashion, centring our
attention on the living
expression of light.
120m^2 of studio space available
for our projects.

Recent clients:
Bitter Kas,
White Horse,
Jané,
Gaggia,
Generalitat,
Pepsi,
Caixa de Tarragona,
G.P...

10 The Pallant
Havant
Hampshire PO9 1BE
England

Tel: (0705) 476624/470310
Fax: (0705) 473851

Contact: John Plimmer

Large studio offering 10 x 8
formats down. Five specialist
photographers backed by E6
and B/W in house facilities.
Separate, permanent and
fully equipped kitchen with
its own studio for food
photography. Location work
undertaken anywhere – try
us. We are good, fast and
experienced.

pinkbarge

Agent:
Pink Barge
Flat 1
23 Crawford Street
London W1H 1PJ
England

Tel: 071-486 1053
     071-487 2639
Fax: 071-935 2417

★ *Phil Rudge*

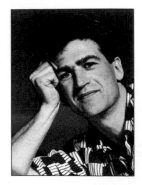

5 Coombe End
Whitchurch Hill
Pangbourne
Berks. RG8 7PD
England

Tel: (0734) 843071
Mobile: 0860 341784

Specialising in:
Portraiture, documentary,
reportage photography.

Clients include:
Haymarket Publishing,
Unilever PLC, Ford,
Peugeot, Digital,
Peat Marwick McLintock,
Channel 4 and
American Express.

★ *Graham* Seager

45-47 Clerkenwell Road
London EC1M 5RS
England

Tel: 071-608 2729

Specialising in:
Interiors
Roomsets
Locations

★ **K***im Sayer*

2 Alma Studios
32 Stratford Road
Kensington
London W8 6QF
England

Tel: 071-937 4231

Studio and Location
Photography

Experienced in:
Organising photographic
shoots in U.K. and abroad for
corporate and advertising
clients.

Clients include:
Alfa Romeo
Athena International
British Gas
Britax
Business Magazine
Case
Cementation (Oman)
Condé Naste Traveller
Courtaulds
Dialcard
Daihatsu
Eurotunnel
Renault U.K.

★ *Peter Seaward*

Tel: 071-231 5485
Fax: 071-231 5487

London agent:
Sue Allatt
Tel: 071-274 8552
Fax: 071-274 8032

Europe agent:
Jenny Garrett-Smith
Tel: 071-229 1658
Fax: 071-221 7185

Paris
Tel: 49 95 06 91

Jamaica Tourist Board
Ad: David Dally

★ **D**erek Seaward

2/4 Vestry Street
London N1 7RE
England

Tel: 071-253 3109
Fax: 071-490 1317

Agent:
Paris
Christian Marguerie
Studio Cosmos
7, Rue Sentou
92150
Suresnes
Tel: 45-06-18-80

SEA BREEZE

★ **D**avid Seed

Unit B
6 Sillavan Way
Salford
Manchester M3 6AE
England

Tel: 061-835 1902
Fax: 061-835 1028

Area of expertise:
Still life, advertising,
special effects,
drive-in and
overhead shooting facilities.

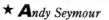
★ *Andy Seymour*

82 Princedale Road
Holland Park
London W11 4NL
England

Tel: 071-221 2021
Fax: 071-792 0702

★ *John Shaw*

190 Haverstock Hill
London NW3 2AL
England

Tel: 071-794 0255/6
Fax: 071-433 3925

In a studio perched above
Belsize Park Underground
I shoot a wide range of
inventive and often
humorous images featuring
people, still life and sets.

Arcade picture courtesy
of JCB.
Amusement machine made
by Mike Shepherd.
Chair made by Paul Baker.

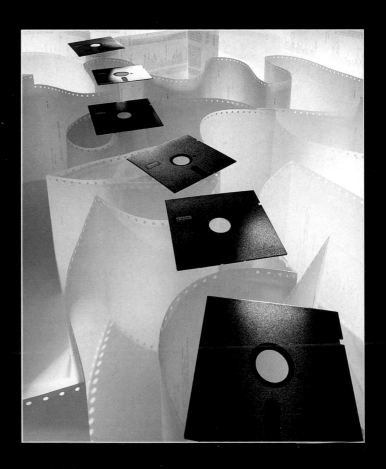

★ *G*eoff Smith

The Old School
1 Thirsk Street
Ardwick Green
Manchester M12 6HP
England

Tel: 061-273 7489
Fax: 061-274 3449

Microwave shot
Client: Brother.
A/D: Simon Broadbent.
Agency: Bowden Dyble
Hayes & Partners.
Home Economist:
Linda Maclean.

Water Shot
Model: Melonie Anne.
Stylist: Jennie.

★ *Duncan Smith*

14A Rosebery Avenue
London EC1R 4TD
England

Tel: 071-837 6873

★ **D**avid Stewart

26-27 Great Sutton Street
London EC1V 0DF
England

Tel: 071-608 2437

Agent:
Noelle Pickford
Tel: 071-584 0908

★ *Michael St Maur Sheil*

Represented by:
Susan Griggs Agency
17 Victoria Grove
London W8 5RW
England

Tel: 071-584 6738
(Home) 036787-276
Mobile: 0860 508679
Fax: 071-584 1732

Annual reports, corporate
portraits, industry, location,
travel and aerials.

Clients include:
Allied Steel & Wire,
Bentley Woolston,
Charter Group,
Chembank,
European Travel & Life,
Exxon,
The Jenkins Group,
Mobil,
National Geographic,
Reader's Digest,
RTZ,
Shell,
Taylor & Ives,
Tor Pettersen,
Unilever,
Ultramar,
Westall Tomkins.

1. *Fireproof Cladding.*
2. *Travel & Leisure.*
3. *RTZ.*

★ **A**nnie Stone

6 Reveley Square
Surrey Docks
London SE16 1HS
England

Tel: 071-252 1095

Editorial and
Corporate
Portraits

Editorial and commercial
fashion and beauty.

Extensive and impressive
client list available on
request.

★ *G*raham Tann

26/34 Emerald Street
London WC1N 3QA
England

Tel: 071-405 7900
     071-831 9877

Still-Life, Corporate and
Cars.

Clients include:
Renault, Lotus,
British Telecom, Courage,
Mathers, The Salex Group
and B.E.T. Companies.

British Telecom

★ **D**avid Timmis

Tel: 071-833 4482

★ *John Timbers*

61 St. James's Drive
London SW17 7RW
England

Tel: 081-767 8386

Area of expertise:
People.

Clients include:
British Airways,
United Biscuits, Abbey Life,
B.O.C., Southern Electric,
D.N.C., Tate & Lyle,
Powell Duffryn,
Harpers/Queen
and 7 Days.

Picture credits:
Title: 'Madge'.
Client: Southern Electric.
AD: Charles Palmer.
Agency: Harrison Cowley.

★ **P**hil Trost

53-55 Bayham Place
London NW1 0ET
England

Tel: 071-383 2073
Fax: 071-383 2109

Client: PA
Art Direction: Stephen Charlton

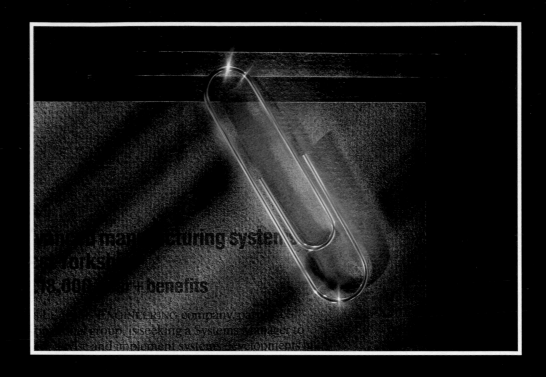

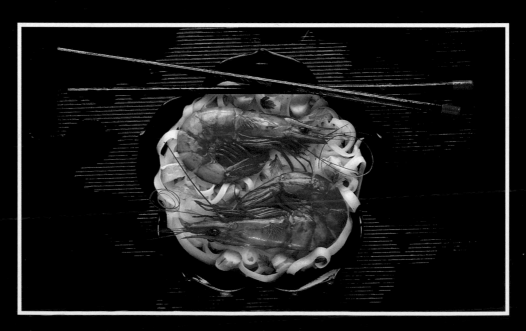

★ *Simon Warner*

Whitestone Farm
Stanbury
Keighley
West Yorkshire BD22 0JW
England

Tel: (0535) 44644

Landscapes

All types of location work for
editorial and advertising.

★ *Pedro Usabiaga*

28004 Madrid
Fuencarral, 16, 1
Tel: 5217681

75014 Paris
32 Bis, Av Rene Coty, 6
Tel: 43352408

33133 Miami
2655 S. Bayshore Drive, AP.605
Tel: 8587723

Best photo in b/w in the
International Festival of
Fashion Photography
in Trouville (France)
September 1989.

'We East of Eden'

★ **M**ike van der Vord

Havelock Studios
2 Havelock Terrace
Battersea Park Road
London SW8 4AR
England

Tel: 071-627 0463

Mike's work ranges from
magazine editorial to
advertising and mail order
catalogues. He has his own
fully equipped studio which
is situated in Battersea and
there is free parking right
outside. Mike is very
experienced at organising
and shooting foreign
location trips as well as
studio photography. He also
enjoys working with both
children and babies. His
portfolio demonstrates the
full range of his expertise
and is available on request.

★ *Paul Venning*

Tel: 081-789 5868
Mobile: 0836 738842

Dewe Rogerson/Water Privatisation

Dewe Rogerson/Water Privatisation

★ **P**eter Waldman

10A Belmont Street
London NW1
England

Tel: 071-485 7798

★ **S**truan Wallace

The Studio
16 Gibraltar Walk
London E2
England

Tel: 071-739 4406
Fax: 071-739 8784
Mobile: 0860 737303

Area of expertise:
Food, drink and still-life.

*Name of logo background
painter stylist:*
Judy-Middleton White.

Name of model: Regina from
Sara Cape Models.
Make-up artist: Ronit from
International.
Name of hand-model: Tonya
from International.

*Name of courvoisier art
director:* Garth Robbins from
T.S.M.

Personal

The Sales Machine

281

★ **S**imon *Warren*

Tel: 071-253 1711 (Studio)
Tel: 0836 322711 (Mobile)
Tel: 071-248 1622 (Fax)

Areas of expertize:
Architecture
Interiors
Industry
Map Reading!!

Page layout by:
Alan Stockbridge

Addison

★ *Simon Warren*   Tel: 071-253 1711 (Studio)

East Midlands Electricity/ Oakley Young

★ *Malkolm Warrington*

14 Emerald Street
London WC1N 3QA
England

Tel: 071-242 4966
Fax: 071-831 1619

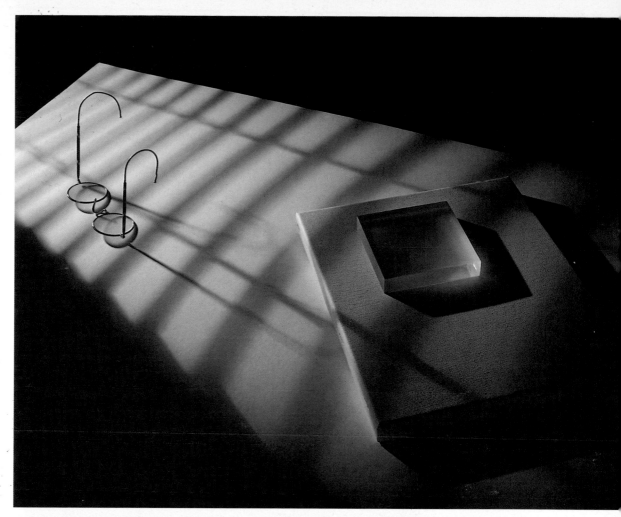

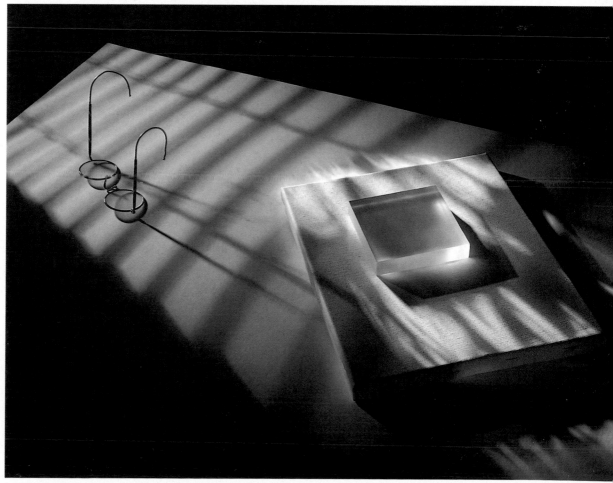

© Malkolm Warrington.

★ *Paul Webster*

2C Macfarlane Road
Shepherds Bush
London W12 7JY
England

Tel: 081-749 0264
Fax: 081-740 8873

Clients include:
Asda,
Marks & Spencer,
Tesco,
Sainburys,
United Biscuits,
Jacobs,
Batchelors,
Nestlé,
Heinz.

*And also many still-life clients
including:*
Mappin & Webb,
Gucci,
Carvela,
Du Pont,
Lloyds Bank,
National Westminster Bank,
Richard Ogden,
C&A and many more.

*Garlic shot for portfolio,
vegetables for Lloyds Bank
Horticultural services.*

★ **P**eter Wedgewood

35 Chatsworth Road
London NW2 4BL
England

Tel: 081-451 1027

People
Location
Corporate

★ *Matthew Weinreb*

The Studio
16 Millfield Lane
London N6 6JD
England

Tel: 081-340 6690
Fax: 081-341 0441
Mobile: 0860 219629

France: 62 65 21 43

I specialise in photographing
architecture, interiors,
landscapes and cityscapes,
though my work has
encompassed a fair bit of
portraiture as well. My
clients include advertising
agencies, design groups,
architects, interior
designers, PR companies
and magazines.

★ *Philip* West

18 West Central Street
London WC1A 1JJ
England

Tel: 071-836 0885
Fax: 071-240 3992

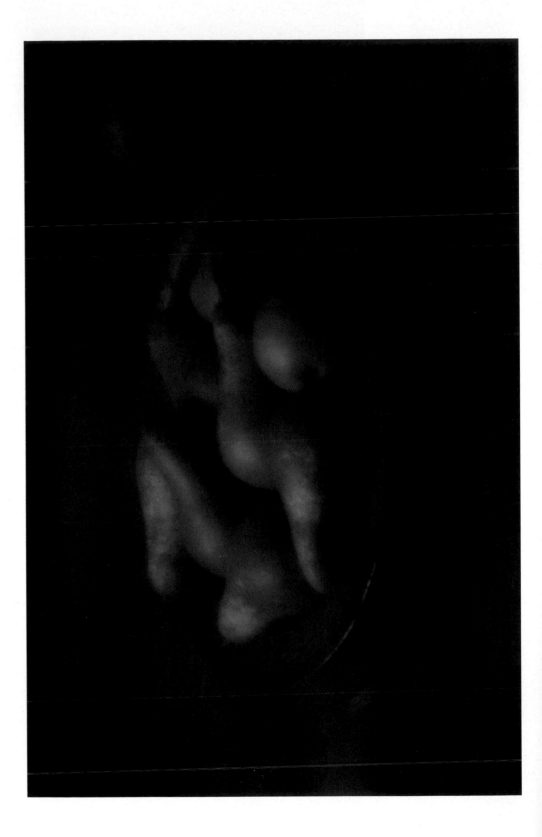

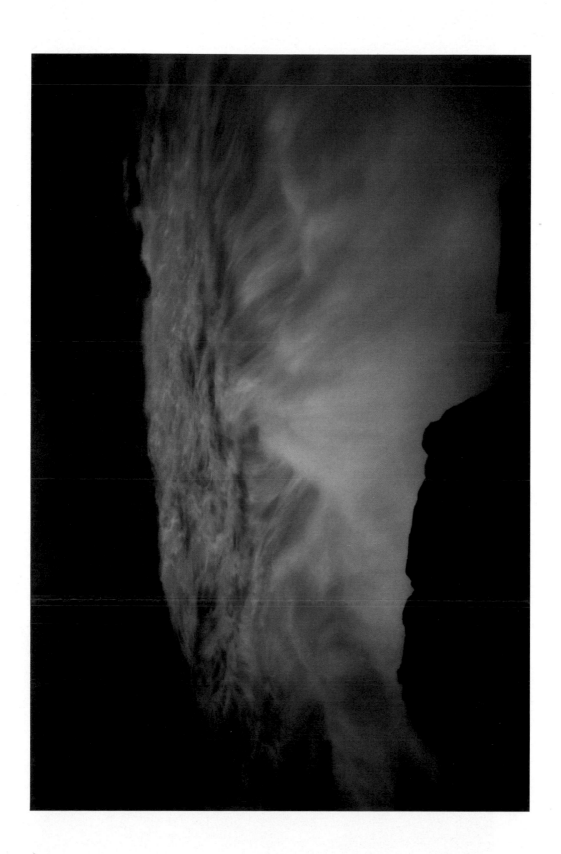

★ *Harry Williams*

4 Brookside Close
Greenacres
Caerphilly
Mid Glamorgan CF8 2RR
Wales
U.K.

Tel: 0222 861331
Fax: 0222 861331
Car phone: 0836 663432

Agent required.

Recent clients:
Ogilvy & Mather (Denmark),
Valin Pollen Group,
Leo Burnett (Hong Kong),
British Tourist Authority,
Chase Bank,
Hitachi,
Wimpy International,
Everest,
Automobile Association,
IPC Magazines.

Top and bottom right:
Art director: Else Prior.
Client: British Tourist
Authority.
Agency: Ogilvy & Mather
Direct.

★ *Peter Williams*

4 Rossetti Studios
Flood Street
London SW3 5TF
England

Tel: 071-352 5334
Fax: 071-351 2214

Agent in Paris:
Catherine Gromaire
Tel: (1) 47 81 09 10
Fax: (1) 47 84 88 97

Still-life, studio and location.
Worked in France and
Spain.

Art director:
Jean-Francois Dufay.
Agency: Lintas, Paris.
Client: William Grant & Sons.
Model maker: Michael Sinclair.

7 Sedley Place
London W1R 1HH
England

Tel: 071-629 1552
Moble: 0836 371851

Represents:

Kenneth Gilliam
Jonathan de Jongh
Jhon Kevern
John H. Weldon

Jhon Kevern 071-731 7438

Maggie Wise

AD: Tony Homan.   Agency: S.P.A.

Client: Emperor Group.   AD: Que Design

★ **A**dam Woolfitt

Represented by:
Susan Griggs Agency
17 Victoria Grove
London W8 5RW
England

Tel: 071-584 6738
Fax: 071-584 1732

Corporate and editorial
people and places
worldwide; travel,
architecture, panoramics,
aerials and photojournalism.

Clients include:
Country Life,
Esterson Lackersteen,
European Travel & Life,
The Guide Book Company,
Liz James,
National Geographic,
Smithsonian,
Telegraph Magazine,
Thistle Hotels,
Travel Holiday
U.S. News & World Report.

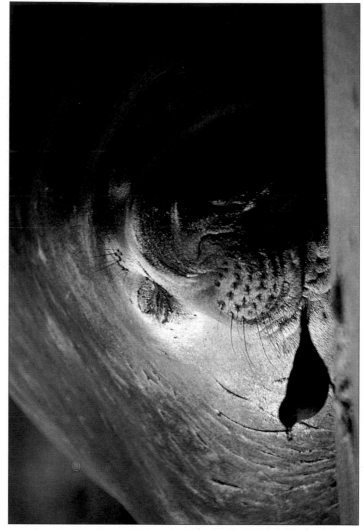

2. *Telegraph Magazine.*

1. *Self.*

3. Esterson Lackersteen.

4. Liz James Design.

Studio 2
George Leigh St School
George Leigh Street
Manchester M4 6AT
England

Tel: 061-236 1285
Fax: 061-236 9621

Area of expertise:
Anything but food.

★ *N*ick Wright

6 Mandeville Courtyard
142 Battersea Park Road
London SW11 4NB
England

Tel: 071-622 5223
Fax: 071-720 9656

*Both photographs taken from
recent books:*
Daphne Du Maurier
Enchanted Cornwall
Michael Joseph: Pilot

Village London Then and Now
Paul Hamlyn: Pyramid

★ **S**imon Yeo

Tel: (0860) 216575

Area of expertise:
Other peoples' problems.
See also pages 306 and 307
Contact 5.

Unit D
Gladstone Industrial Estate
Denmark Street
Maidenhead
Berks SL6 7XJ
England

Tel: (0628) 75242/773256
Car phone: 0836 226750

Food
Still Life
Location
Special effects
Plus some people and animals

This series of shots:
Client: Primary Contact
Art director: John Prior
Stylist: Penny Crawford
Set: Pilot Models

end of professional section

"give us a break"

The colleges featured on the following pages are all affiliated to AFAEP.
The Association of Fashion, Advertising and Editorial Photographers.
Many of the students whose names appear in the credits will shortly be
working in these areas of professional photography.

Kodak Limited is proud to have helped bring these pages into being,
and the work of these students to your notice.

Blackpool & Fylde College

Cheltenham & Gloucester College

Cleveland College of Art

Harrow College of Faculty of Art

Kingsway College

Manchester Polytechnic

Napier College

Newcastle Upon Tyne College

Paddington College

Plymouth College of Art

Richmond Upon Thames College

Kent College

Southampton Institute

Salisbury College of Art

Staffordshire Polytechnic

Stockport College of Technology

Watford College

West Glamorgan Institute

Robert Ashton

Photographic Division
Palatine Road
Blackpool FY1 4DW
England

Tel: (0253) 293071

Contact:
Geoff Clark or
Roger Goodwill

Our continued commitment to quality education aimed squarely at the needs of the market continues to receive your support.
Our thanks to the agency's, company's and publications who have backed up their confidence in us by commissioning our students.

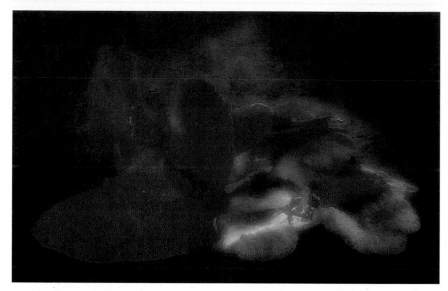

Carl Pinnington

Mike Buckley

Ian Southern

nne Kennils

Andy Montgomery

r Marchetti

Paul Storey

Melinda Thompson

David Corfield

Jeremy Smith

Mike Redfearn

Paul Whitehead

resa Hayhurst

e Wainright

Paul Zammit

★ *Cheltenham & Gloucester*
College of Higher Education

School of Photography
Media Centre
Brunswick Road
Gloucester GL1 1HS
England

Tel: (0452) 426619

The H.N.D. course at
Cheltenham and Gloucester
College is entirely devoted to
Editorial and Advertising
Photography and has strong
links with AFAEP and many
London studios.
Sixty per cent of the course is
concerned with practical
projects which have a clear
purpose but allow for individual
interpretation.
Professional Studies and an
Overseas Project set by a client
or sponsor, are also important
elements in the course.
Students are expected to have a
mature, professional approach
and to be dedicated to a career
in our closen field.

Bruce Sinclair-Jones

Green Lane
Linthorpe
Middlesbrough
Cleveland TS5 7RJ
England

Tel: (0642) 821441
Fax: (0642) 823441

Please contact:
Alan Hampson
course co-ordinator.

The Department of Design Studies offers two courses:
BTEC National Diploma in design (television, film and photography);
BTEC Higher National Diploma in design (communications);
offering options in photography, graphic design or illustration.

On both courses, students are encouraged through a structured programme to develop a strong visual awareness and an ability to become more perceptive. This is also linked with the development of relevant professional and business skills.

Nick Penrose

Robin Teall

Karen Merner

Karl Southerton

John Herring

Watford Road
Northwick Park
Harrow HA1 3TP
England

Tel: 081-864 5422

Miranda Gavin

Karl Grant

Sarah Jarrett

Graham A Hulme

★ *Kingsway College*

For more information
please contact:
Mac Campeanu
Visual Arts Unit
Photography Section
Sans Walk
London EC1R 0AS
England

Tel: 071-278 0541

The section offers a broad
range of courses in
photography and
photographic laboratory
work.
The pictures shown here are
by students on our B/TEC
National Diploma Course in
Photography and
Photographic Laboratory
Practice. This two year full-
time course is most
appropriate for students who
either wish to progress to
Higher Education, or find
work in a professional
laboratory.
The National Diploma
course offers a broadly
based programme which
concentrates on the craft
and technical skills involved
in professional photographic
practice as well as
introducing students to the
critical and analytic theory
necessary when examining
any aspect of the media or
visual arts.

Portrait of carpenter by:
Sylvia Stevenson.
Women's portrait by:
Marina Sanguinetti.

Faculty of Art & Design
Cavendish Street
Manchester M15 6BR
England

Tel: 061-228 6171 ext 2311,
2313 or 2261
Fax: 061-236 7383

Photography – BA (Hons)
Design for Communication
Media.

Editorial, documentary and
advertising.

Top: Lee Avison
Below: Nisha Patel

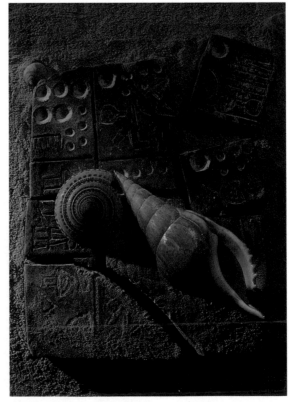

61 Marchmont Road
Edinburgh EH9 1HU
Scotland

Tel: 031-444 2266
Fax: 031-455 7209

The BA Photography course at Napier Polytechnic is one of the few Degree programmes where photography is studied within a professional context. The course also covers other visual media including film, video, slide/tape and graphic design besides Communication, Historical and Business Studies.

Sharon Hogg

Francine Dunkley

Jed Gordon

Sam Seneviratne

★ Newcastle College of Art and Design

Rye Hill
Newcastle-upon-Tyne
NE4 7SA
England

Tel: 091-273 8866

Newcastle College offer a BTEC Higher National Diploma in photography and audio visual media with specialist options in advertising and editorial photography, commercial photography and audio visual media. Housed in a new purpose built building The School of Art and Design lies close to the city centre which hosts many attractions for young people.

Martin Peters

Euan Myles

Paul Spillett

Keith Wright

The School of Visual and
Performing Arts
Amberley Road
London W9 2JJ
England

Tel: 071-723 8826
Ext: 2268

The School of Visual and
Performing Arts at Paddington
College offer a wide range of
full and part-time professional
photography courses.

Richard Poynter
2nd Year BTEC Student

Marisa Battistella second year student
BTEC Diploma in Design (Photography)

Nigel James

Plymouth College of
Art and Design
Department of Photography,
Film and Television
Tavistock Place
Plymouth
Devon PL4 8AT
England

Tel: (0752) 221312
Ext: 5793/5776

The Department offers both BTEC National and Higher National Diplomas in Design (Photography).
These photographs are by final year students on the two year Higher Diploma which consists of a programme of common core skills and an opportunity to specialise in one of three options: Stills Photography; Combined Media Studies; Film and Television.
During both years qualified diving students may study and practice Sub-Aqua photography.
The success of the course is evident from competition results and achievements in the job-market.

Vicky Cornell

Lynne Morgan

Raj Chauhan

School of Arts
Egerton Road
Twickenham
Middlesex TW2 7SL
England

Tel: 081-892 6656

Contact:
Ken Collins Ext 3443
John Feldon Ext 3448

Courses offered are BTEC
National Diploma and
Higher National Certificate
in Design (Photography);
evening only class include
Advanced Colour
Photography and C&G 923.
Specialised 'on demand'
courses in tape-slide, colour
printing and video can be
arranged.

Liz Wilkinson

Steve Moore

★ *Kent Institute of
Art & Design*

Rochester-upon-Medway
College
Fort Pitt
Rochester
Kent ME1 1DZ
England

Tel: (0634) 830022
Ext: 273

Contact:
George Wattson

High National Diploma in
Advertising and Editorial
Photography.
The close proximity to London,
well established contacts with
Adveritising and Editorial
Photographers is reflected in
both students' Industrial
Release and their immediate
post college professional
career.
The 'illustrative' photograph
adjacent was designed and built
in one of our studios.
Committed applicants would be
able to view the studio facilities
by prior appointment.

*Photography by Piet Johnson
Modelmaking Steve Deahl*

★ *Southampton Institute*
of Higher Education

Design Division
East Park Terrace
Southampton
Hampshire SO9 4WW
England

Tel: (0703) 229381

The Design Division offers courses in Fashion, Graphics and Industrial Design, all students study photography, using their skills as designers to attain a high degree of expertise and professional practice. The Division's accommodation looks out on very pleasant parkland in the very heart of the city with easy access via the M3 and M27 motorways, intercity rail links and continental ferry ports.

Mark Abbott

Sood Sudhir

Howard Towey

Sebastien Dragon

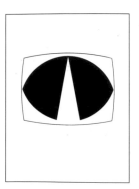

Tomorrow's Image Makers
Department of Photography
Southampton Road
Salisbury
Wiltshire SP1 2PP
England

Tel: (0722) 26122

Salisbury College of Art's
Department of Photography
is educating Tomorrow's
Image Makers. The
Department's reputation
within the visual
communication industry is
based upon its ability to
produce skilled and
motivated graduates. Such
reputations are hard won
and are the result of years
spent maintaining and,
indeed, raising standards.
The courses on offer at
Salisbury occupy a
three-year period of full-time
education. Specialist
facilities in video, film and
tape/slide production exist
alongside stills-based
studios. Students have the
option of specialising across
any of these areas.
Upon graduation, these new
image makers will trade
upon, and themselves add
to, the College's reputation.

Martyn Mackie, fashion, contact College

Simon Winson LBIPP, advertising 0932 67161

Andrew Testa, reportage, contact College

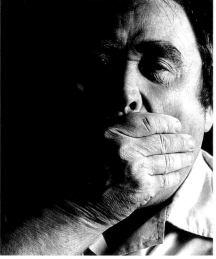

Bernard Manning by Stuart Wood, advertising, people, contact College

Michael Taylor, advertising, contact College

Nigel Rigden, architecture, contact College

Karen Robinson, editorial, features and landscape, contact College

John Falzon, fashion 0722 21603

★ *Staffordshire Polytechnic*

STAFFORDSHIRE POLYTECHNIC

College Road
Stoke-on-Trent ST4 2DE
England

Tel: (0782) 744531
Fax: (0782) 744035

Photography Tutor:
Colin Reiners MA(RCA)

Photography is one of the areas of specialisation within the BA(Hons) design course, one of the largest in Britain. We aim to educate and encourage students to communicate imaginatively and with effect, using photography in its broadest applications.

Students also have the opportunity to extend their experience and abilities into additional design disciplines offered on the course, involving graphics, audio visual and computer aided design.

Graduates enter a wide range of employment, from film production, art direction, to the whole spectrum of photographic practice.

Steve Rowson   contact college.

Faculty of Design
Wellington Road South
Stockport
Cheshire SK1 3UQ
England

Tel: 061-474 3711
(photography)

Course director:
Barry Ainsworth

BTEC National Diploma in Photography. A broad based course but with an emphasis towards advertising and editorial/social documentary photography.
Its aim is to produce thinking photographers with the skills, enthusiasm and commitment necessary to succeed.

Michelle Hughes
contact college.

Jonathan Andrew
01 836 2146

Marina Coles
contact college.

★ *W*atford College

Ansar Admar (0494) 34267

Simon Wagner (0753) 883893

Department of Printing and
Packaging
Water Lane
Watford
Herts WD1 2NN
England

Tel: (0923) 57508
Exts 197, 198

Photography Section:
Ron Southwell, Bob Irons,
Alistair Lamb,
David Whittington-Jones

The Photographic Courses
at Watford College have
been designed to develop
the technical and creative
skills of would be
professional photographers.
The specific aims are to
encourage young people to
understand, interpret and
operate photographically in
conjunction with the other
elements of graphic design
used in the production of
visual communication
material.
It is a learning environment
in which the full implications
of professional, technical
and creative changes in the
photographic industry are
given major emphasis.

Glen Hearnden 081-863 6928

Clive Bartlett (0508) 470240

Graham Lambert (0442) 42382

Lisa Beckman 081-904 5819
081-908 0924

Lawrence Monk (0273) 555128

Vicky Mackay (0923) 34828

★ **West Glamorgan Institute of Higher Education**

Photography Department
Townhill Road
Swansea SA2 0UT
Wales

Tel: (0792) 203482

Course Director:
Ted Gearey Ext. 2243

Tutors:
David Pitt Ext. 2225
Suzanne Greenslade Ext. 2218

The course at Swansea encourages and stimulates work of a highly creative nature within a professional context, specialising in Advertising or Editorial photography, with audio visual, graphic design, technical and professional studies.
The Brecon Beacons, Gower Peninsula and urban and industrial developments provide students with a unique visual resource.

Kevin Bouchier

Darren Fleming

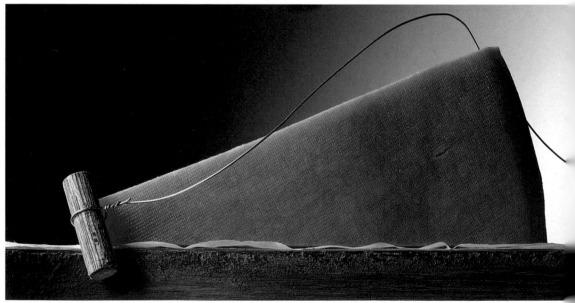

Matthew West

THE PHOTOGRAPHERS' GALLERY

The Photographer's Gallery is the largest and most central institution of photographic art in Britain. It is a meeting place for professionals, for critics, for collectors and for those of us who simply enjoy photography in all its fascinating complexity.

We show a broad spectrum of photography – emphasising contemporary work and a high level of excellence with over twenty exhibitions each year in our three galleries.

The Gallery was initiated by the Director, Sue Davies OBE, in 1971 as the first venue in Britain to be devoted exclusively to photography. We have since grown to include a specialist Bookshop, a Print Room and a reference library. We have a Membership scheme and always welcome new Members, so please call us for details of the different categories.

THE PRINT ROOM at The Photographers' Gallery provides the country's most comprehensive service to collectors and buyers of fine photography. We combine a huge stock – from the most famous names to the newest work – with wide experience in the market and a friendly staff. We sell to individuals, corporations, museums and art galleries.

O. WINSTON LINK *"HAWKSBILL CREEK SWIMMING HOLE, LURAY, VA."*

MARI GIACOMELLI *"YOUNG SEMINARIANS AT PLAY"*

5 + 8 GREAT NEWPORT STREET • LONDON • WC2H 7HY • ENGLAND • TEL 01-831 1772

In the Print Room we recognise that different buyers have different needs, from the corporation which is looking for the smartest art to brighten the office walls, through to the individual making a first tentative purchase after long hestitation. We can answer your queries, provide help on starting a collection, advise on investment, and guide you through the particularities of the photographic market. Even though photographs are reaching record prices in the auction rooms, the purchase of a fine photographic print remains extremely good value for money – and one of the most aesthetically pleasing.

Come and visit us in the Print Room or call Francis Hodgson or Peter Ride on 01-831 1772.

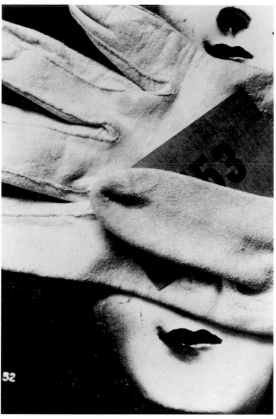

MANUEL ALVAREZ BRAVO *"GOOD REPUTATION SLEEPING"*   MARI MAHR *"13 CLUES TO A FICTITIOUS CRIME"* NO. 5

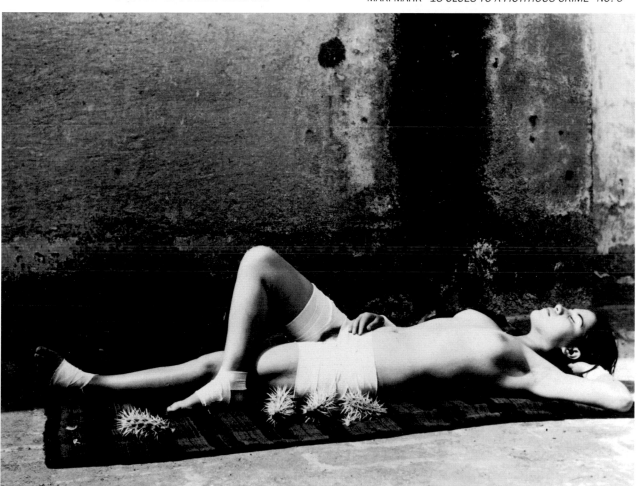

5 + 8 GREAT NEWPORT STREET • LONDON • WC2H 7HY • ENGLAND • TEL 01-831 1772